Advance Praise for
IN DEFENSE OF TROUBLEMAKERS

"Charlan Nemeth has written the definitive
account of dissent and how it affects thinking.
This remarkably insightful, grounded, and accessible
treatment could not be more important or timely."

**—Karl E. Weick, Distinguished University Professor,
Stephen M. Ross School of Business, University of Michigan**

"A lucid, practical guide to fostering smarter teams,
companies, and societies. Charlan Nemeth demonstrates
the power of nonconformists in raising the quality
of our group decisions."

**—William Poundstone, author of
*Are You Smart Enough to Work at Google?***

"A beautifully written and important book
that deserves to be read by the docile and disobedient
alike. Crowds are sometimes wise, but Charlan Nemeth
shows how, when, and why listening to the majority is
dangerous, and why disagreement is often an engine
of innovation, persuasion, and error correction."

**—Adam Alter, bestselling author of
Irresistible and *Drunk Tank Pink***

"Insightful, easy to read, and full of examples. . . .
In this illuminating book, Charlan Nemeth demonstrates
how dissent improves decision-making. This is a book
every manager and board member should read."

**—Professor Saadi Lahlou, chair in social psychology,
London School of Economics**

IN DEFENSE OF
TROUBLEMAKERS

IN DEFENSE OF
TROUBLEMAKERS

The **POWER** of **DISSENT**
in **LIFE** and **BUSINESS**

Charlan Nemeth

BASIC BOOKS
NEW YORK

Basic Books
Hachette Book Group
1290 Avenue of the Americas
New York, NY 10104
www.basicbooks.com

Printed in the United States of America
Originally published in hardcover and ebook by Basic Books in March 2018

First Edition: March 2018

Published by Basic Books, an imprint of Perseus Books, LLC, a subsidiary of Hachette Book Group, Inc. The Basic Books name and logo is a trademark of the Hachette Book Group.

The publisher is not responsible for websites (or their content) that are not owned by the publisher.

Print book interior design by Linda Mark.

Library of Congress Cataloging-in-Publication Data has been applied for.
ISBNs: 978-0-465-09629-9 (hardcover); 978-0-465-09630-5 (ebook)

LSC-C

10 9 8 7 6 5 4 3 2 1

To Serge, Henri, and Len, the "priests" in my life,
for teaching me to care
To Brendan and Lauren, who taught me to love

CONTENTS

ACKNOWLEDGMENTS

THIS BOOK WOULD NOT HAVE BEEN WRITTEN WITHOUT THE influence, over a lifetime, of three professors. This is a deeply personal book, and their influence has been both professional and personal. It is seen in the issues that are covered and the approach I take in thinking about them. Their influence is seen even in my choice of profession. With gratitude, they are cited in the dedication.

Len Berkowitz is responsible for keeping me in the field. I wanted to quit after one year of graduate school, and then searched for possible jobs—and got them—but I still searched for something meaningful. Len found a way to keep me in social psychology. He arranged for a one-year research assistantship with Henri Tajfel in Oxford in the hopes that I would find that meaning. He was right.

I should probably credit Monsanto for keeping me in the field as well. They offered me my choice of two jobs, one as the number-two person in public relations. During the interview with the number-one person, he made it clear that he would offer me the job but advised me to turn it down. He felt that Monsanto would not be able to satisfy my intellectual interests and that I should finish my PhD. He did offer me the job, and I did take his advice.

Henri Tajfel made me care again. A vibrant, brilliant, and sometimes crazy-making Polish Jew who spent five years in a POW camp during World War II, Henri had a sense of important issues, and he set out to solve the heady issues of intergroup relations in particular. Away from my own country for the first time, and finding purpose and excitement in the studies we did, I resolved to continue in research. It was Henri who brought me and Nick Johnson to one of the very first meetings of what would be the European Association of Social Psychology. It was a small meeting consisting of the "chairs" of Europe—and myself and Nick. We were the only students—Henri didn't believe in rules. At that meeting, I met Serge Moscovici.

Serge was to prove to be the greatest influence on my career. Another Eastern European Jew out of the World War II era, he was a true Renaissance man, deeply educated and immersed in everything from the history of science to political science to sociology. More than anyone, Serge understood the potential power of minority voices. I was lucky enough to have a visiting professorship with him and also with Henri shortly after receiving my PhD. The time was prescient. Serge had recently completed the first experimental study of how minority views can persuade.

These three professors were also important to me personally. Len was especially important in the early days. He kept me in the field with his wise counsel every time I considered an impulsive change. He was there for me at difficult times, such as when my mother abruptly died, and at other times as well, such as when I was ready to make a stupid decision. Henri experienced and understood tragedy perhaps more than anyone

I ever knew. And yet, my memories of him always include humor. He was warmly aware of how comical we all are, pumped up with our self-importance. And yet, the conversations were always serious when we discussed social identities, prejudice, and intergroup relations. Over three decades, Serge was the one whose advice I always sought, whether it was on job changes, marriage, or any of the slings and arrows that come our way throughout life. He may be one of the most brilliant and complex individuals I've ever known. No one, in my judgment, understood influence and power better, and he never studied those issues in a vacuum. He convinced me that all research must be applicable to the world around us.

I owe these three professors a great deal. They have now all passed away, Len being the most recent. In fact, he died as this acknowledgment was en route to him. I mourn the three of them.

Among the other professors who have had a significant impact on my thinking and on my professional and personal decisions are Milt Rosenberg, Karl Weick, and Bob Zajonc. They are each special in their own way. Thanks are also due to the wonderful students I have known over the years, including Keith Brown, Cynthia Chiles, Jeff Endicott, Jack Goncalo, Julie Kwan, Ofra Mayseless, Alex O'Connor, Rhonda Pajak, John Rogers, Jeff Sherman, and Joel Wachtler. I thank them from the bottom of my heart.

At a personal level, there are no people more important than my two children, Brendan and Lauren. Both exceptionally accomplished in their own right and independent (to a fault), they are the children I raised. They truly are the ones who taught me what is important and how to love. They are the first to keep me humble, though Brendan's children are showing signs of taking over in that realm.

Writing this book has been a long and reflective process. It was done around surgery, numerous medical tests, and a host of other issues. Through it all, I owe a debt of gratitude to my agent, Max Brockman. From the time he contacted me, he has remained a guiding light. He is a truly good human being, as well as smart, understanding, and extraordinary at his job. And then there is my editor, T. J. Kelleher, who I knew was the "right one" from our very first telephone conversation. He has been invaluable, as has been his assistant editor, Helene Barthelemy.

I must also credit Jonah Lehrer, for it is he who brought me to the attention of Max Brockman by his brilliant coverage of my research in his interviews and books and especially in his *New Yorker* article. And then there is my former graduate student, Alex O'Connor, who was so knowledgeable and helpful in checking the accuracy of the manuscript and the references—and especially in giving me feedback as to what was interesting and what was not. I must also thank the Abigail Hodgen Reynolds Fund and the College of Letters and Science dean at Berkeley, Carla Hesse, for a good portion of the funds to pay Alex.

I am also grateful to the many members of the Northern California chapter of the International Women's Forum for giving me many interviews and support throughout the process. And critically, I want to thank two wonderful doctors who are the smartest and most caring people imaginable. They made me laugh during some dark times. Thank you, Jesse Dohemann and Jacob Johnson.

My final thanks go to all the wonderful cafés in San Francisco that permitted me to sit for long hours over my computer, even when I bought only a few cups of coffee. Perhaps I also owe thanks to Peter Rothblatt, my physical therapist, who took the kinks out of my neck and shoulders from those long periods of concentration.

INTRODUCTION
FEAR CONSENSUS, LOVE DISSENT

THIS BOOK IS FUNDAMENTALLY ABOUT HOW WE MAKE DECI-
sions and judgments. In particular, it is about the influence of others on our judgments. People influence us in
a distinctly different manner depending on whether they
are a majority and have consensus or whether they are a
minority voice expressing dissent. We will see in this book
that a consensus position can sway our judgments even
when it is in error, and even when the facts are in front of
our face.

The more insidious aspect of consensus is that, whether
or not we come to agree with the majority, it shapes the
way we think. We start to view the world from the majority

perspective. Whether we are seeking and interpreting information, using a strategy in problem-solving, or finding
solutions, we take the perspective of that majority. We
think in narrow ways—the majority's ways. On balance,
we make poorer decisions and think less creatively when
we adopt the majority perspective.

Dissent, the minority voice, also influences us. Dissenters, too, can sway us to their opinion. Theirs is an uphill
battle, but they can get us to agree with them. The "why"
and the "how" of a dissenter's ability to persuade us are
very different from how a majority persuades us. Persuasion by a dissenter is more indirect, requires more time,
and follows a more subtle choreography of argument.

Perhaps most importantly, dissent also shapes the way
we think about an issue, the way we arrive at our position
or decision. When we are exposed to dissent, our thinking
does not narrow as it does when we are exposed to consensus. In fact, dissent broadens our thinking. Relative to
what we would do on our own if we had not been exposed
to dissent, we think in more open ways and in multiple directions. We consider more information and more options,
and we use multiple strategies in problem-solving. We
think more divergently, more creatively. The implications
of dissent are important for the *quality* of our decision-
making. On balance, consensus impairs the quality of our
decisions while dissent benefits it.

As beneficial as dissent may be, it is not easy for someone who holds a dissenting viewpoint to express it. When

we think or believe differently from those around us, we are not sure that we are right. In fact, we are prone to think that "truth lies in numbers," and when we find ourselves in a minority we think we must be wrong. Additionally, we are afraid of the ridicule or rejection that are likely to come from dissenting. We hesitate. We put our heads down. We are silent. Not speaking up, however, has consequences. If the individual does not speak up, the group suffers and misses opportunities. Worse, a group compelled to make quick judgments while operating from only one perspective can make very bad decisions. Some are fatal.

> Three days before Christmas, in 1978, United Airlines Flight 173 was headed from JFK Airport in New York to Portland, Oregon, with a scheduled stop in Denver. It was expected to arrive in Portland a little after 5:00 p.m. There were 196 people on board. The crew was experienced. Everything seemed fine. Everything seemed routine.

As the flight approached Portland, the time came to lower the landing gear. Suddenly there was a loud thump, and the plane started to vibrate and rotate. Something was wrong. The crew started to question whether the landing gear was in fact down and whether it was locked. While not knowing exactly what was wrong, they certainly knew that something was not right.

The pilot made what seemed to be a cautious and wise decision. He decided to abort the landing in order to check out the problem and determine the best course of action. The plane was put in a holding pattern.

For around forty-five minutes, the captain and crew diligently investigated the problem and prepared the passengers. Everyone was "on board," so to speak. However, another problem was developing. The plane was running out of fuel. They had more than enough fuel when they left Denver, but they were burning it up while focusing on the landing gear problem. The crew hadn't taken this fully into account. In fact, they didn't calculate how much time remained before they would run out of fuel because they had become blind to this issue.

As the plane ran out of fuel, the engines failed, one after the other. The plane nosed downward and crashed into a suburban area of Portland around 6:15 p.m., only six miles from the airport. The plane literally fell out of the sky. Ten people died—two crew members and eight passengers. Another twenty-three people were seriously injured.

How could this have happened? Not because of any of the "usual suspects." There was no inexperience or dereliction of duty among the crew, nor were drugs or lack of sleep a factor. One important reason the tragedy occurred was that the crew members didn't speak up—or at least, not with conviction. Why?

Real-life situations are always multiply determined. There is never one reason for a sequence of events. Several possibilities come to mind in this case. Perhaps the crew just followed authority, the captain, who was focused on the landing gear. Perhaps the stress prevented them from noticing the fuel level; studies show that high levels of stress narrow attention. Still, when they did notice that the fuel was low, why did they not realize what that meant? Why weren't they aware of the danger it posed? Why did no one speak up?

I would suggest that the consensus itself inhibited the expression of dissent but also shaped the crew's thinking to that perspective. It was not just where the crew's attention was focused that was a problem, but also the information they sought, the alternatives they considered, and the strategies they employed. Once everyone was on the same page, all focusing on the landing gear, they narrowly viewed the situation only from that perspective. They sought information about the landing gear. They considered alternatives only within the context of the landing gear problem. They did not consider the possibility that such a focus had a downside. When faced with information pertinent to another problem—namely, the fuel situation— they failed to fully consider it or to appreciate the growing danger. In fact, they did not even calculate the amount of time remaining before they would run out of fuel. We see the consequences of this thinking in the National Transportation Safety Board accident report's summary of the last thirteen minutes of United Airlines Flight 173.

▶ In the cockpit at 18:02:22, the flight engineer said that they had about "three [3,000 pounds] on the fuel and that's it." They were only five miles south of the airport. At 18:03:23, Portland approach asked about the fuel, and the captain said, "About four thousand, well, make it three thousand, pounds of fuel." About three minutes later, the captain said that they would be landing in around five minutes. Almost simultaneously, however, the first officer said, "I think you just lost number four [engine]." He added, a few seconds later, "We're going to lose an engine."

"Why?" asked the captain.

"We're losing an engine," the first officer said again.

"Why?" the captain repeated.

"Fuel," said the first officer. Almost seven minutes later, the first officer warned Portland approach: "Portland tower, United one seventy three heavy. Mayday. We're—the engines are flaming out. We're going down. We're not going to be able to make the airport."

A minute later, the plane crashed into a wooded section of suburban Portland. United Airlines Flight 173 had plenty of fuel when it left Denver. At the crash site, however, there was no "usable fuel" left. The plane had literally run out of gas.   ◀

"That's it" when reporting a low fuel level of 3,000 pounds? Why did no one shout, "We're running out of fuel!" or, "We're running out of time and need to land!"

Everyone seemed to be in agreement, busily trying to find the problem with the landing gear. Even the captain asked, "Why?" when told they had lost an engine. No one seemed to appreciate the importance of the low amount of fuel remaining because they had only one focus.

Which of us would have thought differently? Which of us would have spoken up? Doing so would have meant challenging the captain and the crew members who were all "on the same page." More importantly, which of us would have even noticed that the plane was out of fuel? When everyone is focused on one thing, they all lose sight of relevant information and options. What we will see in this book is that consensus creates one focus—the group's. It causes us to miss even the obvious.

In this example, most people recognize that dissent could have had value *if* it had been correct. *If* someone had spoken up more forcefully about the diminishing fuel, the crew *might* have paid more attention to it. Even then, we know that people do not always follow the truth. Not only does it depend on who holds the truth, but people are more inclined to follow the majority than the minority, right or wrong. However, what is less recognized is that dissent has value, even when it is not correct.

What we will see in this book is that the value of dissent does not lie in its correctness. Even when wrong, dissent does two things directly pertinent to the example. It breaks the blind following of the majority. People think more in- dependently when consensus is challenged. Perhaps more importantly—and this is the core message of this book—

dissent stimulates thought that is more divergent and less biased. Dissent motivates us to seek more information and to consider more alternatives than we would otherwise, spurring us to contemplate the cons as well as the pros of various positions. I would hazard a guess that had someone on United Airlines Flight 173 challenged the focus on the landing gear, the crew's thinking about other possible problems—including most likely the fuel—would have been stimulated.

I worry when I see colleagues and friends parse their words or remain silent about their objections when they see the presence of the will of the majority. I worry when I watch individuals with a strong need for control at the helm of groups. Whether it is in an organization or a start-up, in a cult or on the board of a co-op building, we see how power coupled with a need for control can manifest itself in hubris and a tendency to silence opposition. Rather than encouraging a culture that welcomes different views, such leaders make sure that dissent is not present—or if it arises, that it is punished. I have even seen board contracts with a friendly "be a team player" provision cautioning new numbers to "respect the collective authority . . . by not undermining majority decisions . . . even when [they] may disagree." The message about dissent is clear. It is not welcomed.

The claims of this book are broad, but I don't want you to take them as pronouncements. I don't want to persuade you through stories, counting on your intuitive acceptance of the claims. I want to persuade you by research facts, drawn from research that has held up over time and in multiple settings.

When I do use narratives, it's to illustrate the range and applicability of the ideas I discuss, informed by the research. They range from the United Airlines disaster to Edward Snowden's revelations about the National Security Agency (NSA), to the Jonestown massacre, to the decision-making procedures of successful hedge funds. My own interviews with CEOs add to the mix. My aim is to help you recognize the patterns of influence in the groups to which you belong yourself and their effect on the quality of your own thoughts and decisions. This book will address the complexity of influence processes and hopefully will cause you to reconsider advice that overestimates the value of consensus and underestimates the value of dissent.

A CHALLENGE TO THE POPULAR VIEW OF CONSENSUS

The ideas presented here contrast with much common advice as well as some popular books, such as the *New York Times* best-seller *The Wisdom of Crowds* by James Surowiecki, which points out the superiority of the judgments of "the many." Although that book is a good corrective to the value placed on the single "expert," the accuracy of large numbers of people is limited. The research supports the relative accuracy of large numbers of people when the task involves common knowledge and the judgments are independent—that is, when people are not influenced by one another. These constraints are important in assessing situations where numbers may provide a statistical advantage. However, the larger concern is that such books can inadvertently give the impression that majorities are likely correct, rather than that they *may* be correct under certain circumstances. This book also serves as a counter to books, such as James Collins and Jerry Porras's *Built to Last*, that link success to cultlike corporate cultures that foster like-mindedness and suppress dissent. Those are the cultures that recommend being a team player, promoting consensus, and being diplomatic (or silent) about disagreements.

This book also contrasts with the work of many researchers of social influence, a field with a long history in social psychology. Social influence is often considered *the* core issue, since it deals with the influence "that people have upon the beliefs or behavior of others." Most of that research has been guided, however, by two tendencies. One is an assumption that influence flows from the strong to the weak, from the many to the few. Thus, there have been many studies of the persuasive power of the majority, but far fewer studies of the ways in which the minority persuades. Though research has now documented the ability of the minority voice to persuade, many in the field still view it as unlikely or assume that it is subject to the same patterns as persuasion by a majority. We will see that this is not correct. The ways in which majority and minority voices persuade others of their position are very different and are manifested in different ways.

The other tendency in the research literature is to reduce the complexity of the ways in which people affect our thoughts, beliefs, and behaviors to one of gaining our agreement. Reducing the broad area of social influence to persuasion is akin to a focus solely on winning—getting people to agree with you, to say yes to you, or to adopt your position. Your coworker doesn't like your preference for a new hire, so you get her to agree with you. You favor a guilty verdict when serving on a jury and convince a fellow juror to vote that way. For decades, social psychologists have studied influence in this narrow sense of persuasion—who, when, how, and why you can get people to agree with you—and used a relatively easy measure for it. If you start out taking position A and I take position B, then your movement from position A to position B indicates that I have persuaded you. Research is easier when we confine it to scales that measure movement from A to B.

But persuasion is different from changing the way someone thinks about an issue, and it's different from stimulating thought. If upon hearing your position on the defendant's guilt or innocence I look at the evidence again and consider the pros and cons of each position and alternative possibilities, you have influenced my thinking. I may not agree with you in the end, but you have influenced how I think and the quality of the judgments and decisions I make. I have engaged in what most researchers consider good decision-making—the kind that on balance leads to better decisions. Did a person standing over the body at the crime scene flee because he was guilty, or did he flee because he was afraid he would be accused? If I consider both options rather than rush to judgment, I am likely to make a better decision. From a research point of view, it is harder to study something like stimulated thought, which is not as easily schematized as persuasion. You have to find ways to measure the information people seek, the options they consider, the quality of their decisions, and the creativity of their solutions. Thankfully, as this book will demonstrate, we have found reliable ways to do this.

If we study only persuasion—that more narrow form of influence aimed at gaining agreement—we don't get to the quality of the decision. We rarely know whether a decision was right or not, since our assessment partly depends on our own values. Was the merger a good idea? Was the majority on a 10–2 verdict correct? Would a 12–0 verdict have been correct? We can't know for sure. In the O. J. Simpson case, which jury was correct: the jury that came to a "not guilty" verdict in the criminal case or the jury that voted "guilty" in the civil case? We all have our opinions on this case, and we all know how clever we can be when we justify our positions. The best way of assessing quality is to instead assess the decision-making process.

We do know something about the process of good decision-making. On balance, a good process leads to a good decision. Good decision-making, at its heart, is *divergent* thinking. When we think divergently, we think in multiple directions, seek information and consider facts on *all* sides of the issue, and think about the cons as well as the pros. Bad decision-making is the reverse. Thinking *convergently*, we focus more narrowly, usually in one direction. We seek information and consider facts that support an initial preference. We tend not to consider the cons of the position, nor do we look at alternative ways of interpreting the facts.

Perhaps you had a grade school arithmetic teacher who taught you to check your work by doing it two different ways. To this day, I don't just add things up the same way a second or third time to check a calculation. Rather than likely repeat the same mistake, I check my work a different way. I subtract one element from the sum to see what remains. I can add up 15 + 28 several times and continue to think it equals 33 (instead of 43). If I subtract 15 from 33, I will see that I made a mistake: 33 − 15 doesn't equal 28. I am then far more likely to look more carefully and find that the sum is 43. By using divergent thinking—that is, approaching an issue from several vantage points—we are likely to make better decisions. This is the kind of thinking that dissent stimulates.

My own recognition of the importance of stimulated thought stemmed from my long-standing interest in jury decision-making. It was in doing research on juries and consulting with lawyers that I came to recognize that influence is far more powerful than persuasion. I also realized that I was less interested in who "won" than in the quality of the decisions reached by juries. I could make money—a lot of it—advising lawyers on how to win by crafting their opening and closing arguments for persuasive impact. I could also show lawyers how to assess the dynamics of a jury in order to know which jurors to remove by peremptory challenge, not just because of their likely vote but also because of their ability to persuade the others. When the focus is on winning, everything is about persuasion—about gaining agreement with the position I favor. However, it became clear to me that my interests were in the quality of the decision—and in justice. Regardless of who wins, is the verdict the correct one?

In our initial studies, my colleagues and I noticed that, when there is dissent, the decision-making improves. Our simulated juries that included dissenters considered more facts and more ways of viewing those facts. This led to decades of research on the ways in which dissent stimulates the way we think, the way we solve problems, and the way we detect solutions. However, we also learned about the power of consensus to stimulate our thinking as well—in diametrically different ways.

We designed most of our experiments to study both consensus and dissent. We predicted and found very different results simply on the basis of whether we were looking at the influence of "the many" or "the few." Moreover, we found the same pattern of results over and over. Consensus narrows, while dissent opens, the mind. Both affect the quality of our decisions. The take-home message of the research and this book is that there are perils in consensus and there is value in dissent.

This message flies in the face of much advice these days. We are told the benefits of liking and being liked, of "fitting in" with the culture. We are taught to believe in the wisdom of the majority and reminded of the likely repercussions of being different, of not "fitting in" or of "speaking up" when we disagree.

Many books, consultants, and academicians echo this advice of "fitting in." Some of it is correct. There are certainly benefits to being liked and to belonging, and there are certainly risks associated with dissent. What is often not reported is that belonging has a price—our agreement. Paying this price often leads to unreflective thinking, bad decisions, and reduced creativity, not to mention boredom, vulnerability, and deadened affect. Have you ever wanted to scream when everyone was pandering and praising each other and no one would talk about the elephant in the room? For example, have you wanted to yell, "Are we crazy to hire this guy?" or, "Should we really be making this merger?"

As the Japanese saying goes: the nail that sticks up will be hammered down. However, too often there is no nail standing up. Consensus prevails, conformity ensues, and group processes look more like groupthink. Ethical violations and problems within an organization go unreported and are not considered. Everyone is walking on eggshells, strategizing and deciding when to speak up and when to be quiet. All the while, we are in these deadening meetings and interactions where many people are often a bit fake—often opportunistic. This isn't the case for everyone, of course. Some genuinely believe in the majority position, but they are still influenced by the incentives to agree and belong. When groupthink takes over, we can lose the value of each individual's input, the experiences and opinions each can bring to bear on a decision or problem. We also lose the stimulating properties of dissent.

Challenging the opinions of others takes courage. I would argue that it also takes conviction to dissent. People don't like it when you argue another position. I myself still get irritated when people disagree with me. If I am honest, I am sure that they are at best misinformed. And I study this stuff. What I do know, however, is that the challenge that they pose makes me a better decision-maker and a more creative problem-solver.

What I also know is that these benefits do not derive from a diversity of demographics (age, gender, race, and so on). Nor do they come from education and training, which, even though well meant, are limited and have benefits that are often overblown. What I have learned is that these benefits accrue from dissent, from being challenged. We benefit when there are dissenting views that are authentically held and that are expressed over times.

THE BLUEPRINT OF THE BOOK

In Part I, we focus on persuasion and the substantial research that helps us to understand how majority and minority views get us to agree with them. I want you to see and worry about the power of the majority, especially when it is unchallenged, for we tend to follow and agree with the majority right or wrong. Too often we assume that truth lies in numbers rather than assess the information rationally. The problem is that we do this unreflectively. We blindly follow the majority. This tendency can be seen in consumer behavior, in ad campaigns, in stock bubbles, and in what we see and believe even in our daily lives.

Even in these situations, I want you to see that dissent provides value. It takes only one dissenting voice to liberate us from the hold of the majority. Dissent makes us better able to think independently, to "know what we know." Dissent can also persuade us, gaining our agreement with its position. We will see that persuasion by dissent is a more artful journey than persuasion by the majority. Considering that people have many reasons to resist agreement with a dissenter, we will see how the clever use of procedures and techniques as simple as varying the order in which people speak can make all the difference for the dissenter's ability to persuade.

Once we better understand how consensus and dissent gain agreement, we are in a position to understand why they stimulate different kinds of thinking. This area, covered in Part II, is where I have spent the greater part of my professional career. We will see detailed research evidence on how consensus and dissent stimulate the ways in which we think and decide, and we will see these processes replicated across experiments and real-life situations such as the Jonestown massacre and Edward Snowden's leak of NSA data.

Part III turns to groups and applications. Groups are complicated, as they involve several people in interaction.

However, scores of studies have uncovered well-established patterns for how and why groups find consensus. Groups often arrive at consensus too soon—and not for good reasons. Some of these patterns are captured by the popular term "groupthink." We will also see the role of dissent in improving group decision-making. Dissent does not just thwart groupthink; it actually increases the quality of the decision-making process.

The message of this book is not that we should *create* dissent, but that we should *permit* dissent and *embrace* it when it is present. The distinction is important, as the most important element of effective dissent is its authenticity, as our research repeatedly underscores. This is one reason why techniques such as playing devil's advocate do not work. They are role-playing and do not challenge bias or stimulate divergent thinking, as does authentic dissent. Authenticity is also a reason why, when brainstorming, rules such as "do not criticize each other's ideas" are ill advised.

When you finish this book, I hope that you will be wary of consensus because you recognize its pitfalls, especially in your own thinking, that you will use mechanisms to reduce automatic thinking, and that you will better recognize the importance of thinking for yourself. As a leader, the hope is that you will better manage group processes and will have techniques at your fingertips to keep discussion open, avoiding premature closure on decisions. Just as important, I hope that you will learn to welcome dissent and not just tolerate it, having come to understand that it has value even when it is wrong.

Above all, I hope that this book persuades you not to suppress dissent. We are all subject to biases and our own prejudices, including our tendency to try to silence those who irritate us by disagreeing with us. However, dissent makes us more complex thinkers. In prompting us to consider the pros and cons of all positions, dissent makes us reconsider our own position, which itself inevitably has cons as well as pros, if we bother to analyze it carefully.

The grand hope of this book is that it will liberate you. One form of this is the liberation to "speak up"—being brave enough to tell the surgeon that he may be operating on the wrong limb, or to tell your boss that his latest plan has a fatal flaw, or to let your best friend know that she is about to buy an expensive dress that is ill suited to her. You will hopefully confront what you think are wrong decisions knowing that, even if you don't persuade the other person, you will stimulate her thinking. You will know that, on balance, your speaking up has improved the decisions and judgments of your groups.

Another form of liberation is to be less afraid to think differently from others. Whether or not you decide to express it, you don't want to lose the ability to "know what you know." Nor do you want to fall prey to the self-brainwashing that often accompanies consensus and a need to belong. Cults know the power of self-brainwashing all too well. So do abusive individuals. There is liberation in recognizing the source of their power as well as your own.

A quote I often use and have always loved comes to us from Senator William Fulbright: "We must learn to welcome and not to fear the voices of dissent." I could not summarize this book more succinctly—unless by adding this remark from Mark Twain: "Whenever you find that you are on the side of the majority, it is time to reform— (or pause and reflect)."

PART I

MAJORITIES VERSUS TROUBLEMAKERS: THE ART OF PERSUASION

GETTING PEOPLE TO AGREE WITH YOU IS AN ART—THE ART OF PERSUASION. It turns out that the majority has an enormous advantage. They almost don't need to try to persuade us. The simple fact that they are the majority is enough for people to agree with them or to follow them. In fact, their power is so immediate and compelling that we follow them even when our own senses tell us they are wrong. The majority has the ability to bend reality.

Minority views, on the other hand, have an uphill battle to persuade us. We don't agree readily. In fact, we find many reasons to resist agreement. Dissenters—"the few"—don't persuade immediately. It has to be done over time, through a choreography of persuasive style. When we do agree with a minority view, it is usually based on a real change in attitude. It means that we now follow or agree with that view because we have been convinced.

1 NUMBERS RULE

THE CLASSIC TV SHOW *CANDID CAMERA* MIGHT NOT HAVE been the most scientific demonstration of the power of the majority, but it was one of the funniest. You may remember this program: Allen Funt did "experiments" on the street and secretly videotaped the reactions of everyday people. One segment from 1962, which I loved, was called "Face the Rear." He had three people (who were paid accomplices) enter an elevator with one innocent rider. Once the doors closed, the three accomplices all turned to the rear of the elevator. When the elevator doors opened, it was revealed that the fourth rider had followed that majority and was facing the rear. After the doors closed again, the three accomplices then faced the side. When the doors reopened, all four were facing the side, although the innocent rider was looking very confused. As this segment continued, the three accomplices removed their hats. The innocent rider did too. When they put their hats back on, he followed suit.

I still show this segment to students, and they still roar when they see it, simply because it gets so quickly to something essential about human behavior. The man in the elevator had no idea why the other three passengers were turning around, but he assumed (as most all of us would) that they knew something he didn't. Perhaps the doors opened at the rear. And so he followed their lead. And even when the door's opening revealed that the majority was wrong—they weren't facing the door, after all—he still followed what the majority was doing.

Majorities have enormous power to get us to agree with them or to follow them. That power is direct and pervasive. We see it everywhere, including in decisions that affect people's lives, such as those made in cockpits or on surgical teams or during jury deliberations. We've already seen that the majority's decision that landing gear was the critical issue caused everyone on the crew of United Airlines Flight 173 to follow and thus to neglect other critical issues. With juries, the outcome of a jury deliberation can be predicted with 90 percent certainty based solely on the majority position on the first ballot. The jury may take hours or days to reach a verdict, but 90 percent of the time its final position is the majority position on the first vote.

That they win doesn't mean that majorities are necessarily correct. Rather, it means that majorities exert im-
mense pressure on our thoughts and feelings, as well as
our judgments and decisions. In fact, as we will see in this
chapter, majorities are so powerful that they can trick us
into believing things that aren't true. Ordinary people,
when faced with a majority opinion that is clearly incorrect, will nonetheless side with that obvious falsehood
over one-third of the time. When the judgment involves
ambiguity—as, for example, questions of politics or business often do—the majority's power is even greater. My
colleagues and I have found that people can follow the
majority as much as 70 percent of the time, even when
that majority is wrong.

The power and pull of the majority is all around us,
even if we don't notice it, and even if we are unaware of
its potential influence over us. Majorities get us to agree.
They get us to follow them, often without reflection. This
is especially true when they are unchallenged. We may
believe that we generally think for ourselves and are persuaded only by strong arguments. But we will see that,
when faced with the opinions of others, we often agree
without good arguments or any arguments at all. We can
even lose sight of what we believe and what we know on
our own. The simple fact that they are in the majority, that
they are "the many," has this particular power to persuade.

Following the majority can make sense if we think that
the majority is right. They *may* be right, and they often
are, but they are not necessarily right. The problem is that

we assume that they are right just because they are the majority. To some extent, best-sellers such as *The Wisdom of Crowds* inadvertently reinforce the assumption that truth lies in numbers.

That book properly points out the value of judgments by "the many" and their superiority in many cases over the judgments of "experts." What may be lost on the reader, however, is that the majority opinion is superior only under certain circumstances. For example, accuracy is more likely found in numbers *if* the judgment is a matter of common knowledge. Judging the number of balls in a jar relies on common knowledge. Knowing who discovered the transuranium elements is not so common; an expert in chemistry is more likely to know the name of Glenn Seaborg than a dozen laypeople. Independence of judgment is another critical element. The average judgment of a large number of people can be accurate provided their judgments are independent. If they have influenced one another, ten people might have the accuracy of one. Herding behavior and stock bubbles, for example, demonstrate that many people doing the same thing is not necessarily an indication of their accuracy or good judgment. They may be following one another rather than making independent judgments.

The problem is not that the majority is wrong. Statistically speaking, they may be right, depending on the task and the circumstances. And it is not that the judgment of "the many" is without value. The problem is that we assume that they are right simply because they are "the many" rather than "the few." The problem is that we make this assumption and then agree or follow—often unreflectively. Thus, while books such as *The Wisdom of Crowds* correctly point to the accuracy of numbers of people over individual people—even over experts under certain circumstances—their readers may not fully appreciate the limits to that conclusion and the circumstances under which it occurs. More importantly, such books may reinforce the assumption that the majority is right.

The majority can often be wrong. What if everyone in your group expressed a judgment that you knew was not true? You might think that you would not care what they said or did and that you would answer correctly, especially if you could see the truth with your own eyes. Research stretching back more than half a century demonstrates quite clearly, however, that the truth is no sure protection against the majority.

The classic study of this phenomenon was conducted in 1951 by the influential psychologist Solomon Asch. In Asch's initial study, individuals were shown two slides side by side. One slide showed a line that served as a standard for the experiment. The other slide had three lines for comparison, one of which was equal in length to the standard line. People were shown a series of these slides. Their task was simply to pick the line that was equal to the standard. This wasn't a difficult task, nor was it ambiguous. One comparison line was exactly equal to the standard, while the other two were noticeably longer or shorter. Alone, people had no difficulty in judging the right answer. It was obvious.

In one of the experimental conditions, the researcher brought in groups of seven to nine individuals, only one of whom was an innocent participant. The others were paid accomplices of the experiment. They formed a unanimous and incorrect majority. The question at stake was whether the naive participant would follow them and give the same wrong answer.

Imagine you are the naive participant. You see the slides. It is clear that line B is the correct answer. You hear the judgment of one person saying that it's line A. You brush him off; maybe he just has poor vision. Then a second person says, "A." Now you start to perk up. A third says, "A." This continues. They all say that A is the correct answer. Now it's your turn. What would you do? Asch's results showed that around 37 percent of judgments agreed with the majority's incorrect judgment.

This study, while first conducted half a century ago, has been replicated many times and in many countries. Whether in Fiji or the Netherlands, in Japan or Canada, many people follow the erroneous majority even when their senses tell them the majority's judgment is in error. This occurs with many different kinds of people and in many different cultures. This occurs whether we are experts or novices.

The amount of conformity, of following a majority's erroneous judgment, is affected by a number of variables.

In general, the amount of following is higher when the task is more difficult or more ambiguous; it is also higher among individuals who have low self-esteem or who are attracted to the group. Even the size of the majority has a bearing on the degree to which we follow them. Most research shows that conformity increases as the majority size increases from one to around three or four; thereafter, size corresponds little to the amount of conformity.

Solomon Asch, like many psychologists who followed in his footsteps, was not simply interested in manipulating situations to increase or decrease the magnitude of this effect. He wanted to know why people follow the majority even when the majority is in error. Interviews with Asch's subjects have revealed—and the subjects of many similar experiments since Asch's study have corroborated—two main reasons why people follow the majority. One is an assumption that truth lies in numbers—that, as the old song goes, "Fifty million Frenchmen can't be wrong." We call this the Fifty-Million-Frenchmen Principle. The other reason is a desire to belong—or conversely, a fear of being different and of inviting ridicule or punishment. Many people can relate to the Japanese proverb that the nail that sticks up gets hammered down. And so it does, leading to the Keep-Your-Head-Down Principle.

In the early study by Asch, the majority contradicted reality and the information that participants saw with their own eyes. After the study, the naive participants were interviewed. Some insisted that the majorities had been correct. They actually believed—or reported they believed—that they had seen the lines the same way as the majority. Others had followed the majority even though they *knew* the majority was wrong. These participants—who were relatively few in number—said that they didn't want to be different. Most participants didn't see it this clearly. They didn't know for sure. They said that they made a judgment call.

Most of the individuals in Asch's study *assumed* that the majority must be right and that the problem was with themselves. Each of them, after all, was a minority of one. We generally think that truth lies in numbers. After all, how could so many people get such a simple task wrong? Because of this assumption, participants no longer trusted the information from their own eyes and believed that they must have missed something or miscalculated. The *average* amount of conformity to error may have been 37 percent, but a much larger proportion of the participants in Asch's study—75 percent—made such an assumption *at least once* during the study. That is, on at least one of the trials, three-quarters of the participants followed the majority error even when it contradicted the information they could see with their own eyes.

Perhaps the more striking finding came from the other 25 percent—those who never followed the erroneous majority, not even once. Even though they answered accurately every time, they, too, were not untouched. Even they reported that the majority was *probably* correct. They, too, didn't really trust the information from their own eyes. They just felt that it was their obligation to call it as they saw it. After all, they were participating in a study of visual perception, according to the cover story.

Some one hundred studies have investigated this phenomenon since Asch, and time and again they have demonstrated the power of the majority. This is especially true when the entire majority is in agreement or when they are all doing the same thing. Like most of us, they wanted to belong. More importantly, they feared rejection, ridicule, or worse. Indeed, that fear may be an even more potent reason for following a majority than any assessment of its accuracy. When we are motivated to believe that the majority is right, it is much easier to arrive at that conclusion.

The history of the financial industry also reveals the power of the majority to shape judgment and behavior. From the original investing bubble, the South Sea Bubble of the early eighteenth century, to the NASDAQ and housing bubbles of the last twenty years, investors have been known to herd—to put their money where others have already put theirs. Empirical work by economists confirms that investors often follow the decisions of others instead of doing their own due diligence. For example, in the late 1990s, there was a large bubble in the US stock market. Between 1995 and 2000, the NASDAQ rose *fivefold*. Prices rose precipitously during that period, only to fall by just as much—in less than a year. Obviously, when the bubble is expanding, people are making money. When the bubble pops, most of those people lose money.

As the economist Robert Shiller argues, bubbles are not necessarily evidence that all those investors were incapable of being rational about investment choices, even as they were making bad investment choices. They were being rational about something else. John Maynard Keynes would describe what they were doing as a "reputational calculation." In this view, one reason why investors follow the crowd and ignore their own judgment is that the average reputational risk for contrarian behavior is greater than the average financial risk. If you deviate from the crowd, you lose in reputation whether you succeed or fail. It is a lose/lose situation. If you are right—and are thus a successful contrarian, it only confirms that you are rash. If you are wrong, and are thus an unsuccessful contrarian, you will be vilified.

This fear of being in the minority manifests itself in workplaces as well. For example, Kathleen Ryan and Daniel Oestreich have found that around 70 percent of employees don't speak up when they see problems. Their research suggests two reasons. One is that employees think that speaking up won't matter and the company will simply ignore what they say. The other reason is fear of the majority—fear of those who remained silent and did not report the problem. This is clearly the fear of repercussions, such as ridicule and rejection by colleagues or a larger audience. Silence then becomes part of the power of the majority.

We see similar kinds of following in consumer behavior. Why do we go into restaurants that are full and avoid ones that are half empty? Why do we follow the star system on Yelp or Amazon even if only thirty people posted a rating, or even if we suspect the reviewers received discounts for their positive evaluations? Why do we buy books that are on the *New York Times* best-seller list? Why did I wait in a very long line at the Musée d'Orsay when I could see that there was a much shorter line? We do these things because the majority of people are doing them, and we take that as a signal that a product or an experience has some value or meets some standard. But how often, blindly assuming that the majority is right, do we wait in line or buy something that we later regret? Why do some of us follow fashion trends each year even when we end up wearing a color we don't like, or buying clothes that will be replaced the following year? This phenomenon provides business models and marketing with a powerful tool. It sells—though we will see some of its subtleties when we pit actions against opinions.

A number of businesses capitalize on the Fifty-Million-Frenchmen Principle and the Keep-Your-Head-Down Principle. Companies such as the customer review site Yelp offer ways for potential customers to follow the majority. One way is by providing ratings for businesses. A listed business with a majority of good ratings is likely to attract customers. A business with mostly poor ratings, by contrast, is likely to repel clients. A business with even just a few good ratings is likely to attract customers if the reviewers are in agreement. Amazon's "Customers Who Bought This Item Also Bought" feature provides another ready-made opportunity to follow the herd.

The Holy Grail of book recommendations is the *New York Times* best-seller list—which, research suggests, leads to a bump in sales for books that land on it. Its power comes from the Fifty-Million-Frenchmen Principle. The many people buying a book could well be right, and even if they're not, there is an appeal to belonging—to being part of "what's happening."

Information gleaned from best-seller lists is also important because it shows what people are doing, not just what they are saying or opining. In fact, actions are often more powerful than words. Most hotel guests have seen little cards in hotels asking them to reuse their towels during their stay in order to "Help Save the Environment." Although somewhat successful, these attempts are greatly improved by adding information about the behavior of others. One study showed that adding the statement "almost 75 percent of guests who are asked to participate in our new resource savings program do help by using their towels more than once" resulted in a fourfold increase in the number of guests reusing their towels.

These examples show that majority behavior can be more powerful than persuasive messages in getting people to buy certain things, or agree with certain opinions, or even to act differently than they might otherwise. A 1971 public service ad aimed at reducing pollution demonstrates this power of behavior over messages. The ad featured a Native American actor, Iron Eyes Cody, being moved to tears by littering. This was followed by the message, "People start pollution. People can stop pollution." Considered a highly effective ad, it was named one of the top one hundred advertising campaigns of the twentieth century by *Ad Age* magazine.

Given the poignancy of the ad and the recognition it received, one would assume that it was also effective at motivating people to stop polluting. The ad had an obvious *prescriptive* message: you ought to stop polluting. It also had a *descriptive* message: many people in fact are polluting. Although many viewers (and presumably the producers of the ad) would have found the descriptive message disturbing, it also conveyed additional information: a large group of people (and in the ad, a majority) were polluting. Which message did viewers of the ad respond to? Did they become less likely to pollute, or did they follow what others were doing? As research by Bob Cialdini and his colleagues suggests, this message might not have had its intended effect.

Cialdini and his research team did a controlled study in Arizona's Petrified Forest National Park. The park had problems with theft: perhaps a ton or more of petrified wood was being stolen each month. With permission from the park, the researchers placed pieces of wood along the paths. They also added signs that were either prescriptive or descriptive. The prescriptive message asked people not to remove the petrified wood from the park. The descriptive message told them that many past visitors had removed petrified wood from the park, changing its natural state. Although both messages could be interpreted as meaning, "Don't take the wood," their effects were not the same. Over the five weeks of the study, petrified wood placed close to signs with the descriptive message was five times more likely to be stolen than wood placed close to a sign with the prescriptive message. No matter what the intent of a message is, what comes across in a descriptive message is what the majority is doing.

Throughout these examples and research studies, we have seen the pervasiveness and the power of majority opinion and action. We follow the majority, right or wrong, because we assume that they are correct. We are also motivated to assume that they are correct because we want to belong. We fear being wrong, but we especially fear the repercussions of dissenting. These reasons would not be worrisome if we used them in making a rational calculation—if we weighed them in making a decision to follow the majority. But they are in fact worrisome because we often don't think at all when we agree with majority opinion or follow majority action. We are much more likely to make quick assumptions and to follow blindly.

The fact that a majority holds a particular position is valuable information. They may be right, especially if each individual holding the majority position made an independent judgment and is not simply following the herd. They also may not be right. There are many books and articles on when the majority is likely to be correct. The important issue, however, is not whether we should or should not follow the majority, but whether we are making a considered decision—one based on an assessment of the value of the information. As was the case for bubble investors and the unsuspecting elevator passenger on *Candid Camera*, too often we follow blindly. We "see" the line length that the erroneous majority sees.

Considering that we are social animals, this sounds problematic. There are some relatively easy fixes, at least in certain circumstances—ways we can reduce our fear of being different or our fear of reprisals for going against the majority. One specific way to reduce that fear is through anonymity. For example, interacting over networked computers rather than face to face tends to reduce the amount of conformity to the majority's position. Another way to resist the power of the majority is to make a commitment to a position prior to hearing the opinions of others.

Unfortunately, life offers us little possibility of anonymity—we usually make decisions in meetings, for instance, in person, and among people who know our names. We rarely vote in a private voting booth. Yet, another solution is at hand—encouraging dissent. As we will see in the next chapter, the power of the majority rests on its unanimity. Even one person, a single dissenter can liberate us to think for ourselves.

2 EVEN ONE DISSENTER MAKES A DIFFERENCE

WITH ALL THE POWER OF THE MAJORITY TO GET US TO FOL-
low and agree, especially to do so without our thinking
about it very much, it may not seem obvious that the majority has a weakness. That weakness is their reliance on
consensus, especially when challenged. Therein lies the
power of dissent to liberate us to think independently, to
"know what we know." Unanimity may be the most important variable affecting the majority's power. Just one
person challenging the consensus can break that power
and increase our ability to think independently and resist
moving to erroneous judgments.

FINDING INDEPENDENCE

As we have seen, people assume the accuracy and the propriety of majority views and actions. They also fear the repercussions of not being part of the majority. They thus follow or agree with the majority, often automatically and blindly, even when the majority is wrong.

Breaking this power so that people are more deliberative and capable of assessing the value of the majority view can be accomplished in several ways. As mentioned in Chapter 1, one way is through anonymity, which, in some studies, is accomplished simply by using a board to separate individuals so that they could not see one another. Another method is to have an anonymous or written process for casting votes or expressing any opinions. Such a process effectively lowers people's fear of being in the minority or of suffering repercussions.

Having votes taken anonymously or by written ballot has another benefit. It commits us to recognizing what we believe *before* we learn the opinions of others. Think of a group vote in which the first three people vote the same way. This almost ensures that the other hands will go up in agreement. Suppose, however, that each person writes down his own vote before seeing or hearing how others are voting. In that case, each member of the group will be less likely to follow the majority. When we have already committed to what we believe, we at least have to confront why we are changing our minds if we are inclined to do so. We stop and pause. We think and then we decide what to say or do. If we first hear the opinions of others, however, it changes our reality.

One early and interesting study conducted by Morton Deutsch and Harold Gerard showed the power of such commitment. Individuals gave verbal judgments in face-to-face groups where the majority's judgment was incorrect. This is the same procedure used in Solomon Asch's length-of-lines study. In Deutsch and Gerard's study, however, each participant wrote down his judgment before hearing the judgments of the others. This was done under one of three conditions: (1) the participant's judgment was completely private, and only he could see what he wrote; (2) the participant signed what he wrote and knew that the experimenter would see it; and (3) the participant wrote down his judgment privately (no one else would see it), but on a "magic pad"—a reusable drawing pad with a cardboard backing and an opaque plastic sheet on top that enabled him to erase what he wrote by lifting the plastic sheet.

You might expect that any version of commitment to what you see or believe would lessen the likelihood that you would follow a majority that was wrong. You say to yourself, *I know that I answered B.* So when the others all judge A to be correct, you should then have to confront the fact that your initial judgment was different. This should make it more difficult to mindlessly follow. That is close to what occurred in the study, but not exactly.

Ask yourself what you would predict. Which form of commitment would increase independence? The public commitment (condition 2)? The private commitment (condition 1)? The "magic pad" commitment (condition 3)? Most people predict that public commitment, one that others will see, would reduce conformity the most. That is not what Deutsch and Gerard found. Public commitment was no better than private commitment—the one where only the participant knew what he wrote down as his initial position.

What may be most surprising is what they found with the "magic pad" condition. You might think that writing down your judgment on paper would not be any different than writing it on an erasable pad and then erasing it. You still know what you believed in the beginning, prior to hearing the opinions of others. Yet the two conditions are different. There was significantly more conformity to error when participants could erase their initial judgments. It was as if participants in the "magic pad" condition could forget that their initial position was different. Such is the slipperiness of judgments when there is a strong motivation to agree with the majority.

So one take-home lesson is that any commitment to what we believe before hearing the opinions of others should be registered on paper, not on an erasable pad. The lesson is larger than a device for voting, however. It is to impress upon you how easily we don't "know" what we believe once we are faced with majority opinion. Just as we can erase our position with an erasable pad, we can just as easily erase our opinion from our own minds. This experiment shows how automatically and unreflectively we follow the majority. Confronting what we believe on the front end—at least pausing and asking ourselves why we would change our opinion—is a buffer against such blind following.

Even better for breaking the hold of the majority so that we think for ourselves is to break the source of their power—consensus. Asch's early length-of-lines study provided evidence that breaking consensus is the route to independence; if the individual had an ally, he was much less likely to follow the erroneous majority. That makes a certain amount of sense. An ally gives us confidence and courage, agrees with us, and supports us. With someone on our side, we are better able to speak up. More importantly, we are better able to know what we know.

What may be more surprising is that having an ally is liberating not because of their support but because the consensus is challenged. What if the dissenter is not your ally? What if she's wrong, even more wrong than the majority? You would probably think that she would be of no help. However, the evidence shows that, even here, we are liberated. We are more independent. With any break in unanimity, the power of the majority is seriously diminished.

To illustrate from the length-of-lines study, suppose I see line A as correct on my own—and in fact line A is correct. It is clearly equal in length to the standard one. When alone, I make no mistakes. Now suppose everyone in my group judges line B to be correct. All the evidence shows that I am likely to agree that line B is the correct answer—at least one-third of the time. But suppose there is one individual who thinks that line C is correct. Like the majority, she, too, is wrong. And she is no ally because she doesn't agree with me. However, she does not agree with the majority either. The group consensus is challenged. In this case, I am far more likely to see what is correct, to know it, and to say it. I say, "A is correct." Even if a dissenter is wrong, and even if she is not an ally, she is of major value because she breaks the majority's power. In that study, agreement with the erroneous majority dropped from 37 percent to 9 percent. Dissent, even when wrong, increases our independence.

THE RISKS: IT TAKES COURAGE

It may take "only one" to break the hold of consensus and raise the independence of thought. However, we know that people fear being that "one." They worry about ridicule or punishment. But is this realistic? Would not people applaud their independence and courage?

The powerful reality is that people get very upset when confronted by dissent. It doesn't require the drama of challenging a government or powerful interests, as Edward Snowden and Jeffrey Wigand did in taking on the NSA and the tobacco industry, respectively. Even on trivial issues, people become angry when a minority view is voiced, even more so if it persists. We argue with dissenters, questioning their intellect, their motives, and sometimes even their sanity. We often respond with punishment or ridicule. It also doesn't take confrontation with power to invoke anger. Simple opposition to "the many" can lead to these predictable reactions, even on issues that are hypothetical or of little importance.

In the preceding chapter, we saw that one reason why people easily agree with the majority is because they fear ridicule and rejection if they disagree. If you are asking yourself whether this fear of rejection is warranted and whether, instead, you would be admired for standing up for your beliefs, the research is not encouraging.

In a now-classic experiment, Stan Schachter studied the reaction to a dissenter. He asked small groups of individuals to deliberate a hypothetical case of a juvenile delinquent. They were asked to come to an agreement on how best to handle him. Their choices varied along a 7-point scale where 1 was a "completely love-oriented" approach and 7 was a "completely discipline-oriented" approach. What they didn't know was that an accomplice of the experimenter had been placed in the group as a dissenter.

In this study, the delinquent child was sympathetically portrayed. Johnny Rocco was poor and raised by a caring and diligent but overwhelmed single mother. He was continually in trouble at school and occasionally with the police. He had little support and few role models, with the exception of his parole officer. From pilot-testing this case, the researchers knew that almost everyone would favor the love-oriented end of the scale, usually position 2 or 3. The dissenter, a single individual, espoused position 7, advocating severe discipline. The reaction?

Two important sets of results from this test have stood the test of time and been repeatedly replicated. The first has to do with communication. The dissenter was the recipient of most of the communication during the task, and it increased as he persisted in his dissent. Eventually, he was cut off. Initially, however, everybody was talking to him. More precisely, everyone was grilling him.

Rather than being an experimental phenomenon, this reaction appears in any group, whether a social group or a business one, and regardless of the issue. It is so consistent that we have used it in classes for decades as a demonstration. Once you express a position different from the majority's, the queries start. The bodies turn to face you. You are asked numerous questions on why you take such a position. Your questioners imply that you are wrong simply because your position is in the minority. You are under attack. Bear in mind, however, that there is a positive side to this. During this grilling, you have the floor, at least until they cut you off. This provides an opportunity to argue your position since you are the focus of attention and communication.

The second set of results dealt with rejection of the dissenter. He was not liked. In fact, he was the least desirable group member. Why? He was in the minority. He challenged the majority opinion. Group members later assigned each other to various roles. The dissenter was relegated to a "Correspondence Committee" that would be responsible for performing menial tasks. He wasn't a contender for the more powerful "Executive Committee." Guess who was the first to go if someone needed to be transferred from the group? The message of this study is that you pay a price for dissent even when the issue is hypothetical or inconsequential. You don't have to confront issues of national security to be punished for holding a minority opinion.

Sadly, nearly *all of us* punish dissent. We don't like disagreement with our beliefs, and we are very capable of inflicting punishment on those who oppose our views when we are in the majority. Whenever I demonstrate the Schachter study in a university class, it turns into a mob scene. Students who are normally polite and tolerant have no trouble laughing at the lone dissenter who takes the "hard line" on the juvenile delinquent. He is clearly wrong. He may even be pathological, and he is certainly cold. Even when I use other issues, even when the dissenting position is soft as opposed to hard, students have the same reaction. Dissenters are rarely liked. The majority will try to convince the dissenter to change and, if unsuccessful, will reject him. To be sure, dissent has the potential to draw a range of reactions—sometimes confusion, occasionally respect or envy. But most often the reaction to the dissenter is irritation and ridicule.

For this reason, daring to dissent takes courage. What is interesting, however, is that this courage, when summoned, is contagious. Dissent can actually increase the likelihood that others will also show courage when faced with consensus in another situation. It is another form of liberation. Dissent can increase the likelihood that we will speak up.

We looked at this possibility in one of our own studies. Dissent did prove to be contagious. Perhaps more accurately, we found that people have the courage to express dissent once they have witnessed it—that they can model a dissenter's courage even if they don't agree with her position. In witnessing dissent, they seem to be reminded that their actions should mirror their beliefs.

In one condition of our study, participants in groups of four had a dissenter in their midst. In judging a series of blue slides on color and brightness, the dissenter was instructed to maintain that every slide in the series was green. In fact, not only were the slides blue, but they were clearly blue, and the participants saw it that way. Predictably, they thought the dissenter was in error. They didn't follow her. In a control condition, participants made their judgments alone—that is, without hearing the judgments of the others in the group.

After the blue-slides task, each person was brought to an individual cubicle, with other people in adjoining cubicles. This was a new group for them. They were now shown a series of red slides. Again the participants had to judge the color and brightness of each slide they saw. All slides were red. When alone, the individuals saw the color as red and, when asked to speak into a microphone, said, "Red." Alone, they did not make mistakes. In the experimental conditions, however, all three of the others in the group said that each of the slides was orange. It was a typical conformity setting. What happened? If participants had no prior experience with dissent (that is, if they were not in the condition where they heard a dissenter call a blue slide green), they were very likely to follow the majority to error. In fact, the results showed that 70 percent of their responses were "orange" rather than "red."

If, however, participants had experienced consistent dissent in the prior setting, the results were quite different. Remember, the dissenter had repeatedly judged blue slides to be green. That dissenter was wrong, and the other participants disliked her. She also had not convinced the participants to judge the slides as green. Yet witnessing her dissenting behavior led to independence in the second setting. They were willing to dissent. Now, when faced with consensus that red slides were orange, participants stuck to the (correct) judgment that the red slides were red. And they said so. Compared to the 70 percent of participants who had followed an erroneous majority in declaring the slides to be orange, only 14 percent of participants did that if they had witnessed dissent in the previous task. We might describe dissenters as attention-getting or foolish, we might question their accuracy or even their sanity, but dissenters often free us to speak up.

In the next chapter, we will investigate the power of dissent to do more than thwart consensus or to liberate us to "know what we know" and give us the courage to say what we know. Dissenters can win—that is, they can persuade members of the majority to adopt their position. We will see that the process is very different when it is a dissenter rather than a majority trying to persuade us. Persuasion is an uphill battle for a dissenter, and the basis of its success has more to do with conviction than with being liked.

3 DISSENT AS AN ART IN CHANGING HEARTS AND MINDS

AS WE SAW IN THE LAST CHAPTER, DISSENT ENTAILS RISK. IF you dissent, you will get attention. You will have the floor, at least for a while. You will be questioned and pressured to change your mind. You will be reminded that you are in the minority, with the implication that you are wrong. You are likely to be disliked and even rejected.

At that point, many of us start to conclude that dissent is not worth it. We ask: *Why do this? Why not stay silent?* Is it futile to speak up if we hold a minority viewpoint? Even if we recognize that we could help others to think more independently, can we ever prevail? Can we actually persuade others? Can we get them to agree with us if we are one of "the few" rather than one of "the many"? If so, how?

The early studies in social psychology on the topic of influence assumed that it was the majority and not the minority who persuaded others. Thus, they studied dissenters only as the target of influence, not the source of influence. Being the target of most of the communication was seen by most researchers as one of the risks of being a dissenter. The dissenter was pressured. He was rejected. Yet those researchers never asked whether the dissenter changed the minds of the majority.

We have many examples of dissenters who have been the center of attention, who have been ridiculed or punished. Yet they persuaded—they convinced us of their position. We see famous dissenters in history, such as Galileo Galilei, who dared to argue that the earth is not the center of the universe, and Sigmund Freud, whose ideas on "unconscious" motives were considered shocking. In their day, these dissenters were reviled. They were punished.

Galileo, for example, was tried by the Roman Inquisition in 1633 and sentenced to indefinite imprisonment, later commuted to house arrest. Some dissenters in history were put to death. Think of Jesus Christ, or of Martin Luther King Jr. Yet no one questions whether they persuaded people. They gained agreement with their ideas. It took time, however—a great deal of time. It took two centuries for the ban of Galileo's "Dialogue" to be lifted and another century before he was formally cleared of any wrongdoing.

During the Victorian era, when women were revered for their chastity and discussion of sexual topics was taboo, Sigmund Freud was talking about the "unconscious" motives, about children having sexual desires toward their parents. He was ridiculed, not permitted to speak at universities, and even considered a sexual "pervert." Some attributed his theories to a cocaine addiction. In the 1890s, his was a minority voice challenging strongly held beliefs. Yet, over a century later, we still see his influence. Concepts like the unconscious or repression or "Freudian slips" are accepted and surface even in popular parlance.

In more recent history, the "wins" by dissenters are often hard to see. Their punishment, however, is clear and immediate. Think of the dissenters who "disappeared" after the Tiananmen Square protests in Beijing in 1989, or dissidents in the Soviet Union like Aleksandr Solzhenitsyn or Andrei Sakharov. Think of Malala Yousafzai, the young Pakistani who survived the Taliban's attempt to murder her for espousing educational rights for women. Think of Jeffrey Wigand, the whistleblower who took on the tobacco industry, as featured in the 1999 film *The Insider*. That film vividly portrays the financial and emotional toll—including harassment, stalking, and threats—that is visited on those who choose to speak up and defy vested interests. A very recent dissenter has been Edward Snowden, whose still-controversial example demonstrates the risks but also gives us clues as to when and why dissent might persuade people to its position.

▶ On June 6, 2013, Glenn Greenwald, a journalist with *The Guardian* newspaper, broke the story that the US National Security Agency had been secretly collecting phone data from millions of Verizon customers. Where did he get his information? A day later, there was an even greater revelation. Greenwald and his colleague Ewen MacAskill reported on a program named PRISM, a seven-year NSA data mining program that collected search histories, emails, and other data from companies such as Google, Apple, and Facebook. Was PRISM domestic spying? What data were being collected, and for what reason?

The reaction of the public was immediate and fierce—but divided. Some worried about the reach of big government and the intrusion into Americans' privacy. Others worried about the possibility that intelligence leaks could compromise national security. Everyone wanted a "balance" of security and privacy. Yet the search was on for the leaker of this information to hold him accountable. The assumption was that he was probably a highly placed official in one of the spy agencies.

They didn't have to look far to find him. On June 9, 2013, the leaker came forward—on his own. At his request, *The Guardian* disclosed that he was Edward Snowden, a twenty-nine-year-old former computer analyst with the CIA who was a current employee of Booz Allen Hamilton—but not for long. Booz Allen, which enjoyed a $1 billion a year contract with the government, quickly distanced itself, saying that the leaks, if accurate, represented a grave violation of its core values.

Commentators and politicians sought to distance themselves from Snowden as well, an exception being US senator Rand Paul, who simply said that "Mr. Snowden told the truth in the name of privacy." Snowden had "no intention of hiding" because he knew he had "done nothing wrong." However, he did run. He was residing in a hotel in Hong Kong, aware of the fact that he would pay a price for his actions. He provided his reasons:

"The NSA has built an infrastructure that allows it to intercept almost everything. I can get your emails, passwords, phone records, credit cards." He added, "I don't want to live in a society that does these sorts of things. . . . I do not want to live in a world where everything I do and say is recorded. That is not something I am willing to support or live under."

Rather than take Snowden at face value, people engaged in a great deal of speculation as to his motives. Was he a hero or a traitor? Those in the hero camp saw him as a man with the courage to do the right thing—as someone who had provided an "incalculable service" and was "prepared to risk his life for his country as a civilian." Critics speculated on his motives, his upbringing, and even his personality. He was variously described as "arrogant," as self-indulgent, and as someone with a "deep character disorder from childhood." A *New York Post* reporter even described him as an "impossibly self-important . . . Kim Kardashian with stubble." Some hinted that he might be a spy.

What ensued had the makings of a spy novel. Edward Snowden was allowed to leave Hong Kong for Moscow on June 23, 2013, in spite of the US request that he be detained and extradited. However, he had to remain in the transit area of Moscow's Sheremetyevo airport, since the United States had revoked his passport. He now had no travel documents, and he had been indicted on espionage charges. Speculation and concern increased, given that Moscow was now in the picture. One country after another, presumably under pressure from the United States, either denied his request for asylum outright or gave an excuse for why his request could not be considered. Some did not respond at all. Eventually, Russian president Vladimir Putin granted Snowden temporary refugee asylum in Russia, an act that angered the White House and some members of Congress.

The bottom line is that whether you view Edward Snowden as courageous or foolish, as a traitor or a hero, he spoke up to power and he paid a price. As of this writing, he is still a man without a passport, without travel documents, and wanted for espionage.

AN UPHILL BATTLE

Did Snowden persuade people to his position? Did other dissenters in history "win"? And if so, why? History shows that many succeeded in gaining agreement. We now know that we are not the center of our solar system. We take for granted that there is an unconscious and that we make "Freudian slips." Millions of people follow the precepts of Jesus Christ. Even Snowden persuaded a number of people that his actions were justified. People agreed with him on the importance of privacy, even when pitted against national security, and agreed that the NSA's surveillance program should be reformed.

There was a sea change in attitudes. People on both sides agreed that Snowden's impact had been enormous—and carried out by a lone individual with a handful of protectors. Not only had the reaction been worldwide, but it had exceeded the "wildest expectations" of Glenn Greenwald, the journalist who first broke the story.

It took longer for actual policy changes to happen, but in April 2015, shortly before the Patriot Act was due to expire, changes were made. A federal appeals court ruled that the massive surveillance programs were not authorized by that act. Congress rolled back their power. The NSA was banned from collecting and storing telephone records, though the agency could still access data obtained from telephone companies—with a warrant. A year later, we saw Apple Computer refusing a request by the FBI to unlock the iPhone of an assailant in the 2015 attack in San Bernardino, California, in which fourteen people were killed. Apple's argument was that the FBI wanted the company to defeat its own encryption, which could compromise all customers' private information. The concern was that this information would subsequently be vulnerable to hackers and thieves, as well as to "unwarranted government surveillance."

How do lone individuals persuade, whether in the past or more recently? How do they gain agreement with their position? Research shows that a necessary, if not sufficient, condition is that the dissenter be consistent in his position. He cannot capitulate or be inconsistent. He cannot compromise if doing so implies a change in position. This may run counter to the common notion that we should parse our words lest we offend, that we should compromise rather than stick to a position too doggedly, that we should make ourselves likable if we are to be persuasive. Many if not most consultants would argue for the importance of the likability factor, but it is not the basis of the dissenter's ability to change minds to his position.

Many historical dissenters were advised to use some form of appeasement or compromise—and many ignored that advice. Snowden, too, resisted calls to either deal directly with members of Congress or compromise. Instead, he remained consistent in his views and persisted in defending his leaking of classified information. Was his success—and the success of other dissenters throughout history—due to this consistency or achieved in spite of it? Would they have fared better had they taken the advice to compromise, to temper their views?

The first experimental study of how dissenters persuade others to their position was conducted in 1969. It specifically addressed this issue of consistency and gave us some insight into the downsides of compromise. The first author of that study, Serge Moscovici, was a Romanian Jew who arrived in Paris after World War II, poor and acutely interested in politics. His own life had made him aware of the power and perils of authority and of consensus, but it had also provided examples of the power of the outsider, especially one who shows consistency and conviction.

In that first study, a minority of individuals gave a position that challenged the majority view, *and* their minority opinion was incorrect. It was the reverse of the conformity studies by Asch and other researchers in which individuals faced an *incorrect majority*. Here, groups of six individuals were asked to simply look at a series of slides and make two judgments: they were to name the color they saw and to rate its brightness on a scale of 0 to 5. They might say, "Blue 2," for example, to indicate that they saw the color blue and it was slightly dim. There were thirty-six slides, and all were in fact blue. They were the same wavelength, differing in perceived brightness by the usage of neutral filters. It was an easy task. People alone answered quickly and confidently that each slide was blue. That changed in the conditions where there was dissent— an opinion that was held by a minority in the group. It was also an opinion that was wrong. This minority called the blue slides "green."

In one condition, two of the six people called every slide "green." These two were accomplices of the experiment, unbeknownst to the other four. Most people would predict that these two individuals would have no influence. The participants themselves dismissed them as having bad judgment or very poor eyesight, at least according to questionnaires they completed after the experiment. This is not the end of the story, however.

In a second condition, those two individuals called the blue slides "green" two-thirds of the time (twenty-four times), but called them "blue" one-third of the time (twelve times). Did participants still question their judgment or eyesight? Yes, though not quite as severely as they did when the two accomplices repeatedly judged the blue slides to be "green." The question is, which of the two conditions, if either of them, could persuade the majority that the slides were green? Would you ever agree with two people calling a blue slide "green," especially when you have a majority—and truth—on your side? If so, which of the two conditions would be more persuasive to you? Would it be the condition in which they were consistently wrong—that is, they repeatedly called the blue slides "green"? Or would it be the condition in which they took that position two-thirds of the time but were in agreement with the majority and with reality one-third of the time?

Most people think that neither condition would be persuasive. When guessing which condition would be more persuasive, most say the second condition, the one in which the two individuals called the blue slides "blue" one-third of the time and called them "green" two-thirds of the time. The reasoning is that, in that condition, they had at least some credibility. They were correct and also agreed with the others one-third of the time. This prediction makes logical sense, but it is not what the experiment found.

The results showed that it is the condition of repeated "green" judgments that persuaded—that is, when the minority called each slide "green." In that condition, around 9 percent of the majority's answers were "green" as well. When the minority was more correct but less consistent— that is, when they judged the blue slides to be "green" two-thirds of the time and "blue" one-third of the time— they had no influence. In this condition, the majority stuck to "blue," calling the blue slides "green" only 1.25 percent of the time. The take-home message? Repeated but consistent error was more persuasive than some error and some truth.

Researchers found the results surprising, but subsequent research has repeatedly replicated these results. The overriding conclusion is that consistency is what is important. Without consistency, there is no clear position, at least not one held with conviction. Study after study shows that, without consistency, a minority voice does not persuade. However, we will also see that consistency, though necessary, is often not sufficient.

Numerous studies have shown that even with consistency, the minority may not persuade, at least not at the public level. Minority opinion often loses. Research on juries, for example, shows that fewer than 5 percent of verdicts are the position favored by a minority on the first ballot. In our own experimental studies using mock-jury deliberations, there was often no public movement whatsoever to the dissenter's position, even when the dissenter was consistent. The members of the majority do make clear, however, their anger toward the dissenter. More than once, I was asked for "combat pay" by the accomplice we hired to be the dissenter—to offset the distress he endured. In almost every experimental group, he was subjected to the anger of the participants, and occasionally he was threatened. We don't like people who disagree with us, particularly if they are "the few" and we assume, therefore, that they are wrong.

These and other studies that focus on public agreement with the minority position, however, underestimate the extent to which dissenters persuade the majority. Over and over, studies show that dissenters change more minds in private than in public, unlike majorities, which often get public agreement even if people don't believe in the truth of the majority position.

We repeatedly find that people resist showing public agreement with dissenters. Often, however, we find that they have been persuaded privately. When you ask them later, or if you ask them in a way that enables them to avoid acknowledging that they agree with the dissenters, they show substantial attitude change in the direction of what was proposed by the dissent. In one study, the dissenter argued for low compensation in a personal injury case involving torn cartilage. The others did not move publicly to his position. That is, they did not adjust their compensation recommendation—not even by a dollar. In their private judgments of that case, however, as well as in other personal injury cases, they did lower the compensation they thought was appropriate, relative to participants who had not been exposed to a dissenter. We see the same pattern of findings in an experiment described in the next section.

THE ART OF CONSISTENCY AND COMPROMISE

While the importance of consistency is "consistently" underscored in research studies, the concept has been refined beyond a matter of simple repetition. A dissenter can become more artful in articulating his position. Indeed, he can be seen as consistent even if he changes his position, but only in response to new or changing information. He cannot be seen as capitulating. Capitulation renders him ineffective.

With this perspective, it is worth reexamining the lives of martyrs, who, if nothing else, were consistent. They did not capitulate. They were even willing to die for their convictions. Would they have had the same impact had they tempered their beliefs? Would Freud's impact be as significant today, over a century later, had he compromised on his theories? He was in fact advised to compromise, in order to make his ideas more palatable, but he ignored that advice. Would Edward Snowden have been more persuasive had he compromised with the US authorities? The research suggests that consistency is more effective than compromise in changing minds, but what about the extensive research supporting the common advice that compromise is needed to get public movement to your position—to make a deal? If the previously described research is correct—and scores of studies suggest that it is—do you need to be consistent and refuse to compromise to be persuasive? Or do compromise and consistency persuade at different levels?

The Two Faces of Compromise

You may be thinking that it is all fine and good to fall on your sword for your beliefs, but that compromise is often needed. You know that compromise can be effective. Here, we need to make a distinction between changing attitudes and negotiating a deal. If you want to make a deal, you usually do have to compromise, but if you want to change minds, compromise is a bad strategy. As we saw in the blue-green study, compromise that suggests inconsistency makes a dissenter ineffective. In that case, even when compromise was more correct—at least one-third of the time—it did not change minds. What compromise does do is make you better liked—or, more precisely, less disliked. But liking is not the determining factor for a dissenting position to be persuasive.

This gives us some insight into "compromise" decisions made by people who may publicly agree on something that no one believes. It is a way of making a deal, rendering a verdict, or maximizing outcomes rather than changing minds to reach an agreement. To illustrate, a criminal case might have two viable verdicts, either "first-degree murder" or "not guilty," depending on whether you believe an eyewitness. Yet juries will come to a compromise verdict of "manslaughter" in order to gain consensus, even though that verdict does not fit the facts and no one believes it is the proper decision. That verdict illustrates public movement but not private attitude change. For a dissenting position to persuade, could compromise be successful at a public level, or is consistency, as the research suggests, the key to persuasion, whether public or private?

To better understand the role of compromise in reaching an agreement versus changing minds, we did a study that tested the two different lines of research. Negotiation research argues for the power of artful compromise as a way to achieve public agreement—a "deal" in your favor. The other line of research, such as that described earlier, shows that compromise is ineffective at changing attitudes because it undermines the perception that the compromiser has conviction.

My lab attempted to see whether both lines of thought might be right. We started with the hypothesis that compromise is effective at the public level—that people move publicly to an individual who compromises rather than to one who is intractable. On the other hand, we did not expect compromise to lead to private attitude change. Rather, we hypothesized that consistency—intractability—persuades at the private level but is relatively ineffective at gaining public movement to a dissenter's position. Further, we hypothesized that there is a "sweet spot" where the dissenter can have it both ways—where she can get agreement *and* change minds.

We pitted compromise against consistency. In this study, one individual took a minority position involving compensation for a plaintiff. The issue was how much a person should be awarded for pain and suffering from a ski lift accident in a case where a corporation had been found to be negligent. The group was asked to come to a unanimous decision. In ten rounds of discussion, each person gave his position on each round.

There were three experimental conditions, and all of them involved an accomplice, paid by us, who would take a position challenging what we knew would be the other individuals' positions. From pretesting, we knew that the others would favor an award of $150,000 to $200,000. The dissenter would argue for $50,000, a substantially lower amount.

In one condition, the dissenter was consistent. He did not compromise. He stuck with the same position on all ten rounds. In a second condition, he compromised early in the deliberation: he moved toward the majority position on round 2 and then remained consistent. In a third condition, he compromised very late in the deliberation by moving toward the majority position on round 9—at the "last minute."

Compromise, early or late, led to reciprocal public concessions. When the dissenter moved, so did the members of the majority. They were approaching one another publicly. Without compromise, the majority showed little movement publicly. There was a stalemate. Private attitude change, however, showed a different pattern.

The individuals returned a day later and gave judgments on a series of six different personal injury cases. One was very similar to the one they had discussed. The other cases were quite different in terms of the demographics of the victim and the degree of negligence. Their judgments revealed that their private attitudes had changed, but they showed a different pattern than they had in the public movement the day before.

Those who had faced a dissenter who was consistent—who had shown no compromise—had changed their attitudes. The majority had moved in the direction of the dissenter's position and favored significantly lower amounts of compensation. Remember, these were the same individuals who wouldn't budge publicly the day before. For those who experienced a dissenter who compromised early (in round 2), there was no change in their attitudes. They may have moved publicly the day before, but they didn't change their opinions. Their judgments on these six cases were similar to those of a control group who had faced no dissent.

It was the "late compromise" condition that had it both ways—both public and private attitude change. When a dissenter compromised at the last minute, he did two things. He appeared consistent and, at the same time, flexible enough to achieve an agreement. He did not change his position. He simply offered a concession. As a result, he achieved both outcomes. This was the "sweet spot." He got the other participants to make public concessions and he changed their private attitudes.

THE INFLUENCE OF DISSENT: MORE THAN IT SEEMS

The research repeatedly shows that dissenters have "hidden" influence. In general, they change attitudes in private more than in public. They change minds—even if those in the majority don't realize it or choose not to acknowledge the influence.

We see this pattern in many of our studies using mock-jury deliberations. If the dissenter doesn't compromise, agreement is rarely reached. The majority will not budge. They just get irritated. However, the repeated pattern is a change in attitudes, even just ten minutes later and even despite no movement during the deliberation. Participants often don't acknowledge this change directly, but if the researcher changes the phrasing of the question, their response reflects the change in their attitudes. The researcher can ask a million "what-if" questions, such as, "What if the plaintiff asked for double the amount of money?" This gives the majority cover: they can change their minds without acknowledging having been persuaded by the dissenter.

Once we recognize that dissenting views change more minds and hearts than is publicly evident, we begin to understand our power in "speaking up" or being the one person who dares to challenge consensus. We may persuade even if there is no public acknowledgment of it. We have this power not only on important issues but on trivial ones—as illustrated by a small personal experience. On coming to Berkeley as a full professor at age thirty-five, I was prepared for a culture that valued free speech and independence, even protest. Our offices were very plain, even austere. So I decided to put a rug on my floor. That may seem innocuous enough. Much to my surprise, however, I was told in no uncertain terms that all the offices were the same—*for a reason*. Equality seemed to be more highly valued than freedom.

I ignored that unsolicited opinion. I was a tenured professor, so there was some safety in nonconformity. Within a week, I noticed that a colleague had put a carpet on his floor. Then another. Then another. To this day, almost every office has a carpet on the floor. Some have cappuccino machines. Others have walls painted in bright colors or decorated with art. These small experiences remind us that we often struggle to appease or to compromise. We tend to underestimate the power of knowing our own minds and acting on it. We also have to recognize that we will not get credit. I am absolutely certain that no one knows the origin of the rugs on the office floors in Berkeley's Psychology Department.

The private or hidden influence that is characteristic of dissent was evident even in that first experimental study with blue slides. I often refer to that study since it pointed to the most important questions and findings, the ones that have repeatedly been replicated and extended. It demonstrated how dissent can change even what we see, including our notions of what is blue or green. Additionally, it gave evidence of the hidden influence of dissent, for it showed that private attitude change is even greater than what is found in public.

Recall that, in that study, two dissenters called blue slides green, either consistently or inconsistently, and that the consistent dissenter was able to get 9 percent of the majority's public judgments to be green. However, there was another task following those judgments of blue slides.

After the public set of judgments, each individual was given a pile of blue-green colors, the kind that you see in paint store samples. All were "blue-green," but they varied from the very blue to the very green. Each person was asked to place the samples—which were given to them in random order—in one of two piles: a blue pile or a green pile. That was it. Their task was simply to judge each blue-green sample as blue or green. The findings showed that those who had been exposed to a consistent minority, someone who had repeatedly judged the blue slides to be green, altered their judgment of what was blue or green. They put more samples into the green pile than did individuals who had not been exposed to dissent. These individuals, *even those who did not publicly call the slides green*, had changed their notion of what was blue and what was green. The consistent minority judgment, even though wrong, persuaded people far more than the 9 percent of "green" judgments that were made in public.

WINNING WITH RESEARCH PRINCIPLES: *TWELVE ANGRY MEN*

Being persuasive when you start from being alone, or one of "the few," takes more than consistency, and it takes more than conviction—though both are essential. Influence by a minority never happens immediately. It takes time and a choreography that is consistent and persistent but not dogmatic. Unlike majorities, which can win quickly and almost automatically, having a persuasive style is very important for a dissenter to win. The choreography of the dissenter's verbal and nonverbal behavior is important.

Some elements of this choreography over time are well dramatized in the classic film *Twelve Angry Men*. An analysis of it corresponds to some basic research on how minorities persuade—that is, how they gain agreement with the minority position. We will see in Chapter 5 that the film also illustrates another form of the dissenter's influence— stimulating the thinking about the evidence so that a better decision is reached. Here we concentrate on the dissenter's ability to persuade, which is more akin to winning than being a force for good decision-making.

Far better than a long list of experiments and variables, *Twelve Angry Men* demonstrates the *art* of influence, which includes timing, an observation of subtle cues from others, and knowing when to talk and when to listen. Although not wildly popular when it was made in 1957, this film has stood the test of time and is regularly taught in psychology departments and business schools to illustrate the principles of persuasion.

▷ Remarkably simple compared to the special effects and action films of today, *Twelve Angry Men* is the story of twelve men locked in a jury room who are deliberating the case of a young man accused of killing his father by stabbing him. The charge was first-degree murder. The story is the unlikely fable of a lone dissenter on the jury, portrayed by Henry Fonda, who persuades the other eleven jurors to agree to a verdict of "not guilty." That may sound boring, but the film is in fact a fascinating and insightful portrayal of how minority views can persuade. It is also particularly instructive for how to control the process—for example, who speaks first, whether speakers defend their position in order, when new votes are taken, and so on. The take-home message is that, if you control the process, you control the outcome.

The case seems like a no-brainer in that there were two eyewitnesses: one saw the murder directly, and the other saw the defendant fleeing the crime scene. The twelve jurors are anxious to reach a quick verdict. It's one of the hottest days of the year, and the members of this all-male jury are eager to attend a baseball game that night. There is not much to discuss, or so most of the jurors believe. The first ballot is taken by a show of hands. Eleven hands go up for "guilty," some of them reluctantly after seeing the other hands rise. Then comes the slow rise of the hand of Henry Fonda, whose character is an architect. He votes "not guilty," not because that is his position, but because he "isn't sure." A young man's life is on trial, and he at least deserves a discussion of his guilt or innocence. The other eleven are predictably upset. "There's always one" is the opening salvo. The eleven jurors aim their communication at the one holdout, asking him, "How come you voted 'not guilty'?" Again, we see how powerful and replicable are the early findings on reactions to dissent. Fonda is the immediate target of communication—and he isn't liked.

An important turning point comes when the foreman suggests that the eleven "convince this man where he is wrong and we are right." Hubris is out in full force, but such is often the folly of those in power or those who have the numbers. This suggestion changes the usual offensive position of the majority to a defensive one. Rather than press Fonda to defend his position, which we know would likely result in ridicule, each juror now explains his own position. One by one they defend their belief that the defendant is guilty, usually with pronouncements such as, "It's obvious," or reminders that an eyewitness "saw" him commit the crime. It is an open-and-shut case for those eleven.

As each of the eleven jurors gives his reasons, each opens himself to questioning, which exposes the main basis for his belief. When the basis is one of the two eyewitnesses, Fonda repeatedly asks, "But couldn't they be wrong?" As further deliberation ensues, that possibility proves to be important.

At one point, they note that one eyewitness was old and had a limp. They agree on the amount of time that would have elapsed between his hearing the body hit the floor and running to the door to see the defendant descending the stairs. They ask for a diagram of the apartments in the building. Reenacting the testimony, they realize that the eyewitness couldn't have gone from his bedroom to the door in that short amount of time. Doubt has now been raised about a key piece of evidence on which some of their positions were based. Fonda's repeated question "But couldn't they be wrong?" now seems reasonable. The initial assumptions about the eyewitnesses might be wrong.

Having each individual defend his position has another consequence. Their testimony shows the holes in the majority's unanimity. We know that a break in that unanimity will severely undermine the power of the majority. The eleven may agree on the verdict, but not for the same reasons. In the film, they disagreed on those reasons and argued about it.

Each also reveals his certainty—or lack of it. If you are looking for an ally, it is important to notice those in the majority who are unsure. Some jurors showed themselves to be clearly prejudiced, which angered some of the others and provoked arguments. This sets up opportunities for Fonda. For one thing, he knows now who is likely to be persuaded. He knows the power of getting a convert to his position since the essential basis for the power of the majority is its unanimity. Herein lies another advantage of understanding procedural rules.

As mentioned earlier, one procedural decision that proves to be important is having the majority of eleven give their reasons (rather than pummel the dissenter for his). This decision made by the foreman favors Fonda, the dissenter, even though the foreman views it as a way to convince Fonda of the error of his ways. Later in the deliberation, there is another example of the power of controlling the procedure. This time it is Fonda who uses procedure to his advantage, but in a way that requires considerable subtlety since he is not the foreman.

At one point, the jurors seem to be at an impasse. Sensing some uncertainty, Fonda wisely announces that he wants another vote, but this time he wants the vote made privately—in written form rather than verbally. He announces that he himself will not vote. If all eleven vote "guilty," he will not stand in the way. They can stop the deliberation and return a verdict of "guilty." Note that he takes the high road in his suggestion. It is hard to deny him. Note, too, that he does not indicate any uncertainty or change in his own position. He is simply acknowledg-ing the power of the majority and the difficulty of chang-ing their minds. He also understands that a written ballot is more likely to allow a show of independence. He espe-cially understands that if one person is willing to be his ally, that could change the nature of the deliberation. He is guessing that he has that one ally.

Fonda knows that a few of the eleven are wavering— or at least that they are thinking about the case and have indicated some uncertainty. The written ballots are read aloud: "Guilty, guilty, guilty . . . guilty," seven times in a row. Then the foreman pauses for a moment as he reads the eighth piece of paper: "Not guilty." Then "guilty, guilty, guilty." One person has stepped up to the plate. Fonda now has an ally.

When the finger-pointing tries to root out who could
have been this idiotic to vote "not guilty," the old man,
played by Joseph Sweeney, speaks up and says that it was
he. He gives his reasons. It is not that he has changed
his position, but that he is no longer so sure. More so,
he feels that Fonda, in standing up to the majority, has
shown courage and deserves to be heard. Deliberation
now begins again in earnest.

We know the end of the film. One by one, the individuals move and the jury comes to a verdict of "not
guilty.

While a dramatic vehicle, the film demonstrates with
subtlety how minority positions can prevail. It is consistent with available research. That's why the film works.

Initially, we see the power of public voting to apply pressure to conform. The first ballot is a public show of hands.
When asked who favors a "guilty" verdict, the first few confidently raise their hands. The others follow, though some
hesitate. Eleven jurors vote for a "guilty" verdict. Then we
see the difficulty in being the "one," the dissenter. When
asked who favors "not guilty," Fonda raises his hand. He
is alone.

The immediate reaction that we see is consistent with
the research. Fonda is the target of ridicule and communication. "There's always one" is the first reaction, and
everyone questions Fonda. How could he have such a position? Normally, he would be on the defensive, but here

is where a procedural decision changes that dynamic. The foreman suggests that, instead of letting the process take its normal course, each juror should explain the reasons for his position. In other words, members of the majority now must explain why they are voting "guilty." It is the members of the majority now who are on the defensive and, in the process, revealing the flaws in their reasoning and their disagreement with one another.

The value of an ally, especially one who defects from the majority—one who "converts"—is well illustrated in the film. Fonda's character gains an ally through several brilliant observations and procedural moves, which are consistent with research findings.

Fonda pays attention to the verbal and nonverbal behaviors of each of the jurors to discern who is likely to move to "not guilty." When the jurors are close to an impasse, Fonda asks for a ballot—and a written anonymous ballot at that. He knows that a potential ally would be more likely to stand up to the majority privately—when he could do so anonymously rather than in public. Fonda also puts the onus on the potential ally by offering not to vote himself. He agrees to abide by the will of the majority should all eleven ballots be "guilty." This way, the dissenting position of "not guilty" would only remain viable if another juror stepped up to the plate and voted "not guilty." Anyone who was uncertain or moving to "not guilty" could no longer hide behind Fonda, the dissenter.

By observing what people said and did, Fonda knows that the person most likely to become his ally will be

Joseph Sweeney's character. The written ballot is a risk, but Fonda senses that his own persuasiveness has peaked, and he needs an ally to further break the majority's power. His risk pays off: Sweeney joins the dissenting position. He announces that he is the one who voted "not guilty" and gives his reasons. These include admiration for Fonda's courage, a factor confirmed by research findings.

At its heart and throughout the deliberation, the film demonstrates the power of consistency and of being willing to pay a price for one's beliefs. The film shows the "art" to argument and procedure. It is a dramatic demonstration of how the dissenter can persuade the majority. The focus is on consistency and admiration, not on liking or compromise. Fonda is not liked by those with whom he disagrees, but he is persuasive.

To some extent, Edward Snowden, too, is not liked but commands a modicum of respect, even from his critics, including an improbable source. Eric Holder, who was attorney general under President Barack Obama during the time of Snowden's leaks of NSA information, later said that Snowden had performed a "public service" for initiating the changes that had since been made. Of course, that doesn't mean that Snowden will be coming home anytime soon.

PART II

CONSENSUS VERSUS DISSENT: CLOSED MINDS VERSUS OPEN MINDS

GETTING PEOPLE TO AGREE WITH YOU IS IMPORTANT. THAT WAS THE TOPIC of Part I—persuasion. We have seen that "the many" have an easier time gaining agreement than do "the few." There are different reasons for majority persuasion versus minority persuasion. The nature of the agreement varies—for example, majorities gain our agreement at the public level, even without private attitude change, whereas minority voices may convince us at the private level in ways that often are not evident publicly. The majority's persuasion is direct and immediate. The minority's persuasion is often hidden and subtle.

Although persuasion is important, the ability to gain agreement is only part of the story when it comes to consensus and dissent. Part II is about *how* we think about an issue when exposed to the majority view or the minority view, not just whether we agree with the specific positions for which they argue. In my judgment, the fact that majority and minority voices stimulate different thinking in us is far more important than whether they are persuasive—whether they "win" or gain our agreement—for the way we think is what impacts the quality of our thinking and our decision-making.

Majority opinion and minority opinion stimulate our thinking in diametrically different ways. Majority opinion, especially when there is consensus, changes our thinking in ways that are narrow and closed, whereas minority opinion—dissent—broadens and opens our thinking. As a consequence, consensus and dissent have profound impacts on the quality of our decision-making and the creativity of our solutions to problems. On balance, consensus is an impediment while dissent is a benefit.

4 CONSENSUS NARROWS THINKING — AND KILLS RATIONALITY

IN THIS CHAPTER, WE WILL CONSIDER THE WAYS IN WHICH the majority viewpoint shapes the very thought processes of those who are exposed to it. Consensus makes the majority formidable. Just knowing the opinion of the majority is enough to change the way we seek information, how we think about that information, the options that we consider, the strategies we use for problem-solving, and even the originality of our thinking.

We may worry about the power of consensus to get us to blindly follow. However, the more insidious peril of consensus is that it stimulates our thinking in ways that narrow the range of what we consider. In fact, it does more than narrow our thinking—it sends it in one direction. We think from the perspective of the consensus. A number of research studies document these broad claims.

ROUTES TO BAD JUDGMENTS AND DECISIONS

Our own decision-making can go awry when we agree without reflection—that is, when we follow others, right or wrong. As we saw in Chapter 2, we often do this when facing consensus, which can put us on automatic pilot. More importantly, consensus stimulates the kinds of thinking that lead to the *opposite* of good decision-making. We are biased in the information we seek and the alternatives we consider, and we tend not to think about the cons as well as the pros of a position. Consensus even limits our ability to detect solutions that are right in front of us. Consensus produces an intense gravity that narrows our reasoning and warps our perspective to such a degree that we are much less rational actors.

Alone, we consider only a slice of information. We have many biases in how we select and interpret that information, usually in ways that are consistent with our beliefs. We also have biases in the strategies we employ in problem-solving, often using old solutions when they no longer work. However, when we are faced with majority opinion, our range of thinking narrows even more. Worse, our thinking favors one direction—the perspective of the majority. In general, narrow, unidimensional thinking lessens the quality of our decision-making and problem-solving. It even accounts for our complicity in our own brainwashing.

The power of consensus to stimulate single-perspective thinking is one reason why groups make mistakes and bad decisions—even fatal ones—and why cults and cultlike organizations are so intent on—and effective at—creating consensus.

CULTS AND SELF-BRAINWASHING

Cults may seem distant from our lives, but in fact they are simply an extreme version of the type of consensus we see every day. In general, consensus narrows our thinking to the perspective of the majority. We can then start to think of abnormal things as normal and lose our ability to see alternatives or to question the consensus. We even become willing advocates of the majority perspective, thus contributing to the closed bubble of information.

▶ On November 19, 1978, many people awoke to the news that 918 people had died in the South American country of Guyana; 276 of them were children. There were grotesque photos of hundreds of bodies lying on the grounds of the Jonestown cult—or some might say religious movement—called the Peoples Temple. This wasn't a massacre perpetrated by a terrorist, or an army, or a mentally ill individual mowing them down. The evidence is that these people committed mass suicide. They drank a mixture of a grape-flavored juice, cyanide, and sedatives and even gave the lethal drink to their children before they drank it themselves. How could this have happened?

The Peoples Temple was led by Jim Jones, an Indianapolis preacher who arrived in Northern California in the mid-1960s with a handful of loyal followers. His mission, embraced by the times and especially in San Francisco, was equality. His message was about warmth and caring. The Peoples Temple community he formed would be made up of people taking care of one another, far removed from the evils of capitalism and individualism. Of course, he added the usual elements displayed by cult leaders—namely, his own special relationship to God and his ability to perform miracles. For instance, Jones would "heal" cancer patients in front of the congregation.

Jim Jones had a powerful message, and he was charismatic. However, he also understood the power of consensus for thought control. To achieve consensus, he carefully recruited individuals who were likely to "fit" the community and be receptive to his message. He repeated his message continuously. He made sure potential converts interacted with believers. Whole families went to Jonestown and then reinforced each other's decision to be there. Jones encouraged public expressions of agreement, and he did not tolerate dissent. He didn't even tolerate doubt. Friends and family members who didn't believe or follow soon became ex-friends or ex-family.

Any active dissent was punished. Critics or those showing any resistance were regularly brought before the assembled members and chastised. The other members were encouraged to pile on additional punishment. Children, for example, might be beaten in public for resisting or raising objections. This was all for the greater good of attaining a form of utopia, Jim Jones style.

> Jim Jones's notion of a spiritual ideal was to be removed from the evils of capitalism, to live and work together, and to pool assets. The congregation would be removed from daily stresses. Decisions would be made for them, and life would be easier, kinder, more routine, and more equal. They would not need to think for themselves. Jim Jones and his loyal aides would do that for them.

Jones was convinced (and convincing) that the US government would eventually destroy this ideal community. He continually predicted that the government would torture them—and offered mass suicide as the honorable alternative. Members "practiced" suicide, drinking a concoction similar to Kool-Aid but without the sedatives or cyanide. That practice would soon have its opportunity to be put into effect.

That opportunity took the form of US Congressman Leo Ryan visiting Jonestown in response to some troubling reports he had received. He represented California's Eleventh District, near San Francisco, and some of his constituents were concerned that their loved ones were being held against their will in Jonestown. He decided to find out for himself—and brought a television crew with him.

After they arrived at the compound, Ryan and his entourage started to see potential problems. Someone passed a note to a member of the film crew. It named some individuals who wanted to leave. The next day Ryan announced that he would take those who wished to leave back with him. Only a few accepted that invitation. However, Jones and his lieutenants weren't about to permit any defections or challenge to the consensus they had created. At some level, they understood that the dissent by even just a few members would open the floodgates and break their control.

At the airport, while Ryan and his entourage waited for the planes to take off, several armed members of the Peoples Temple shot and killed five people on the tarmac, including the congressman. Jim Jones's prophecy seemed to be coming true. Knowing that there would be repercussions for these killings, Jones now ordered them to do what they had practiced. They prepared a vat of grape drink that now included cyanide and sedatives. Most complied and drank the concoction. Jones did not. He died of a bullet wound to the head, apparently self-inflicted. He didn't drink his own "Kool-Aid."

Most of us, when we learn about tragedies like the Jonestown deaths, wonder why it happened. Why would anyone, much less over nine hundred people, commit suicide? Many of us assume that the reasons lie in the personalities of the individuals, who must have been weak or uneducated or easily persuaded. Most of us think that we ourselves would not have complied—that we certainly wouldn't have taken our own lives on the basis of what a leader and others were saying or doing. Or would we? From the previous chapters, we know that we can't be certain.

In many real-life examples, the consensus involves a combination of people, some of whom might be leaders while others are followers. To be sure, the leader or authority figure can be important in *creating* a culture of agreement, but it is consensus that gives that culture its power. Jim Jones didn't have to continually repeat his message or convince people. Consensus did that for him. As John Stuart Mill recognized, the majority can be a form of tyranny, one harder to recognize than the tyranny of rulers since, in democracies, people identify with the government. The will of the majority can have even more power than rulers, partly because we are not as aware of the pull that it exerts.

There is a reason why organizations like Jim Jones's Peoples Temple create and maintain consensus. There is a reason why cultlike organizations cultivate consensus and reject dissent "like a virus," as described in popular books such as *Built to Last*. As we saw in Part I, majority opinion has a forceful impact on gaining agreement, especially when there is consensus.

Jones understood the power of consensus and carefully cultivated it. He restricted interaction to those who were believers. He removed interaction with non-believers. Anyone likely to dissent was cut off from communication. If someone did dissent or even expressed doubts, she was punished. Consensus was not only desired but mandated. Similar stories are told about Scientology, the Branch Davidians, and other organizations variously referred to as cults or religions. They often use "minders," omnipresent people who report on others' activities to make sure they are not interacting with non-believers or espousing heresy. Minders make sure that there is the appearance of unquestioned agreement.

While the leader can try to mandate consensus, groups are very capable of creating consensus on their own and punishing dissent. We will see the substantial research on this in groups when we get to Chapter 6. However, it is achieved, I would argue that there is real power in the consensus, for it changes how people think. Consensus is not simply public agreement. It is more subtle and more insidious than the power to pummel people into submission. Its greater power is that people think from the perspective of the consensus. They seek and analyze information selectively, in ways that justify that perspective. They become complicit in their own brainwashing. Without even knowing it, they do not see when reality is warped.

Consensus operates powerfully and dramatically—and not just in foreign lands where people are especially isolated and dependent. When the people around us agree, we assume that they are right. When everyone is in one line at the box office, we go to the end of that line. When everyone in the room laughs, we laugh too—often contagiously and unconsciously. In fact, we are often unaware of our mimicry. We are even less aware that we are starting to think like the majority. We may think that we are rational beings just seeking information, but we are not aware of the fact that we are selectively seeking information—information that supports the consensus position.

Biased Thinking and Bad Decisions

If we were to list the ways to make bad decisions, it would include a narrow and biased way of thinking. If you think this way, you don't consider a broad array of objectives or multiple courses of action. You select information that takes one perspective and you concentrate on the pros of that position, avoiding consideration of the cons or of alternatives. You filter everything through that perspective. This is a good way to make bad decisions.

This is what happened in Jonestown, but not because of coercion. Peoples Temple members were thinking from the perspective of the consensus. A number of research studies support the likelihood of that occurring.

The first step in decision-making is the search for information. If you want to make a bad decision, you begin with a narrow search for information that corroborates a single preferred position. Majority opinion is often enough to stimulate this biased kind of search. Rather than search broadly, you actively seek information that will corroborate and thus convince you of the truth of that majority position. A study that we conducted at UC Berkeley illustrates this.

Students in groups of four or five believed that we were studying student attitudes on some proposed changes in campus housing policy. The proposals included segregating floors by gender, having mandatory curfews, and assigning roommates based on college major. We knew that students would hate these potential changes. They did.

These groups of students were then given the results of a survey showing that a majority of students—around 80 percent—favored the changes. In addition, the experimenter mentioned that the present group showed a similar pattern, with four of the five favoring the proposals. Each student thought that she was alone in opposing the proposals.

While waiting for the next phase in the experiment, the students were given the opportunity to read additional information on the housing issues. They were not required to read anything. However, if they wished to, they could read comments from the survey. They could select up to twelve articles that were either short (half a page) or long (three pages of detailed comments) and that either favored or opposed the proposals. The average number of articles selected was well over four. More important was what they selected to read.

Those who believed that 80 percent were in support of the proposals wanted to read the comments made by members of that majority. They selected more articles and more pages favoring the proposals than opposing them.

They wanted the detail. They wanted to understand the perspective of that majority. They showed much less interest in reading the other side of the issue, which, by the way, was their own position.

It may look like a long stretch from Jonestown to university dormitory proposals, but the important point is that, even when the issue is less important, we think from the perspective of majority opinion. Our thinking is narrow, more so than when we are considering something on our own. It is also more biased. We take the majority's point of view, not our own. We selectively seek information that corroborates the majority position.

Many of the reasons for this biased search for information are the same reasons why we follow or agree with a majority. We start with an assumption that the majority is correct or knows something we do not. We also want to belong. Seeking information that corroborates the majority position is one way to do this—to corroborate the majority position and to belong. Imagine how much greater was that motivation for those who were thousands of miles away in Guyana in 1978. Everyone was apparently in agreement. "It was good to be in Jonestown." Imagine their fears if they had doubts or found themselves forming a minority view, especially after witnessing others being ridiculed or punished. There was consensus, there were no opposing views, and there were fears of punishment for even harboring doubt.

In some ways, the experimental results are even more remarkable because they occurred in the absence of the kind of power and control exerted by a cult-like organization. They occurred without interaction, and without a leader. They occurred even when the issue was inconsequential. Simply knowing the majority position is enough to shape and bias the search for information. We don't just follow the majority position; we willingly search for information that corroborates it. And we narrow our search, excluding other information—even information that would support our initial position. We become complicit in our own brainwashing by the majority.

Dramatic cases like Jonestown—in which an uncontested belief system led to mass suicide—show the consequences of creating and maintaining a single perspective. From the outside, it may appear difficult to understand why someone would permit others to dictate decisions regarding their finances or parenting—and certainly their lives. It is more easily understood when you realize that this occurs over time—in small steps. An invite is followed by a dinner, which is followed by participating in many social events with like-minded people, which is followed by moving in with members, by moving to a different country, and so on.

The process is not unlike seduction. Each step involves a commitment. The first commitment might be as small as accepting a drink or sitting down for a conversation. With each commitment, it is easier to escalate to a date, to moving in, to pooling assets, and so forth. For cults or cultlike organizations, however, the individuals' willingness to cede control over basic personal rights is due, in part, to the uncontested consensus within the organization. This may be the most important technique in the cult's toolbox.

Most of us are not in cults or groups that are as extreme as Jonestown. However, it is worth reflecting on the fact that many of us live in information bubbles characterized by consensus. We may have been raised in one, even if we were unaware of it. Our religious or cultural or political upbringing may have included only friends, classmates, and family who were in ideological agreement. Though perhaps not as closed as a true cult, such an upbringing is similar to it. We add to the bubble by choice—our choice of friends or news outlets that agree with that upbringing. We end up creating and living in a world of relatively like-minded people that, like Jonestown, can lead to strongly held shared beliefs and a lack of reflective thought about their downsides.

Biased Focus and Problem-Solving

Much like decision-making, problem-solving usually benefits from multiple approaches. If we take only one approach to a solution, we had better hope it is the right strategy or at least the best one. If the crew of United Airlines Flight 173 had considered several approaches to the problem, they probably would have thought more carefully about the level of fuel. As we described in the introduction, that certainly would have been better than concentrating on a single strategy that focused only on the landing gear. Going back to the arithmetic example, taking only one approach often leads to repeating the same mistake. You can add up

12 + 19 several times, but if you first think it equals 21, you might continue to believe that. If, however, you take another approach as well—subtract 19 from 21—you come up with 2, not 12. You realize that you made a mistake.

Taking multiple approaches is a first step. It doesn't ensure that you will find the correct solution, but it greatly increases the likelihood compared to taking a single approach. Luckily, the wisdom of a solution or decision is often reasonably apparent once you consider multiple possibilities and seriously analyze each.

When a majority uses a particular strategy, we tend to use it *simply because* it is the strategy of the majority. The majority strategy may not be based on success or even a good likelihood that it will work. Yet we follow it. Worse, we tend not to use other strategies, even ones we would normally use on our own. Thus, we don't just follow the majority—we think like them. This can be an especially pernicious consequence of majority opinion, as we are not generally aware of this kind of influence.

One of our experimental studies demonstrated this. The task involved anagram solutions. Individuals in groups of four were asked to write down the first three-letter word they noticed when a string of letters was briefly shown. They saw the letters for less than a second. Imagine a quick flash of a letter string like "rTAPe." Everyone sees the word "TAP," since this is the word in capital letters from left to right, the direction in which we read. For five different letter strings, each individual wrote down the first word she noticed. And as we expected, each person wrote down the word formed by the capital letters from left to right. With the letter string shown for so little time, that was all they could see.

We then gave participants feedback, but it was not true feedback. After collecting their answers, they were told what the four of them first noticed. Using the example of the letter string "rTAPe," they were told that their answers were "PAT, PAT, PAT, TAP." Each person believed that the other three people in the group first noticed the word "PAT," the word formed by the backward sequencing of the capital letters. The same kind of feedback was given for all five slides. For example, having been given the letter string "wDOGa," they were told in the feedback that their group saw "GOD, GOD, GOD, DOG." Each participant knew that she had seen "DOG." This meant that the others all saw "GOD." Now came the test.

Each person was given a series of ten new letter strings and asked to write down *all* the words they could form from the letters. They had fifteen seconds for each letter string. What did they write down? Did they form words differently than people in a control condition who had received no feedback about how the others answered? The answer is yes. In forming words from the new letter strings, they took the perspective of the majority, adopting its strategy. They couldn't have told you that was what they were doing, but that was the way they formed words. They used backward sequencing to find words.

The majority had consistently seen the word formed by the backward sequencing of letters. Now the participants were trying to form all the words they could from a new series of letter strings. Let's take an example. Suppose I give you the letter string "nRAPo." Try to come up with as many words as you can. Now take a look at how you formed those words. You could use forward sequencing to form words from left to right, the way we read, to get words like "NAP," "RAP," and "NO." Or you could use backward sequencing to get "OR," "PAN," and "OAR." You could also use a mixed sequencing to come up with words like "NOR," "RAN," and "APRON."

Results showed that individuals used the majority's strategy to form words from the letter strings. They found *more* words using the *backward sequencing* than did people in the control condition who had received no feedback. They did not find more words overall, however. Their formation of more words using backward sequencing of letters came at the expense of finding words using forward sequencing. Exposed to the strategy of a majority, they focused on that way of solving problems. Their focus became narrow, lessening their ability to use other strategies and find other solutions, even ones they would have used on their own, such as forward sequencing.

FOCUS CAN BE A LIABILITY

In both decision-making and problem-solving, we find that majorities stimulate a narrow focus from the majority perspective. In general, a narrow focus is a liability and leads to bad decisions, for we limit both our search for information and the alternatives that we consider. It leads to poor problem-solving, for we limit our strategies as well. In most situations, limiting ourselves this way is detrimental. We don't think about the complexity of the situation or seriously consider alternatives to the majority focus. We may not even look.

One study demonstrates this tendency to not "see" solutions when a majority judgment goes unchallenged. This is similar to what happened when the United Airlines crew ignored the fuel level while focusing on the landing gear. In this study, the task was determining whether a stick figure—a one-armed "hanging man" kind of figure—was embedded in a larger drawing. Participants were shown six more complicated figures that might contain the hanging man image; it could be on its side or upside down. The task was to find which of the six figures contained the hanging man image. In fact, three did contain the hanging man and three did not. One was very easy to detect.

People in small groups of six were asked to do this task, and four of the six participants (a majority) in each group were accomplices. Those four each made the same two choices: the easy one and one other. In one condition, that second choice was correct; the figure contained the hanging man. In another condition, the second choice was incorrect: it did not contain the image. It turns out that it didn't matter if the majority was right or wrong. People followed them anyway—and followed them exactly. They picked the exact same two solutions, whether they were right or wrong.

What is more important is their inability to find the hanging man image in the four other figures, those not chosen by the majority. Two were correct. However, the participants did not detect those solutions. Faced with majority opinion, they appeared to focus on the figures selected by the majority and did not even look carefully at the other figures. They were unable to find the other correct solutions. What they did do was follow the majority, not just the majority's opinions or strategies, but in the focus of their attention.

FROM CULTS TO COCKPITS

If you are going to take a single perspective when approaching a problem or decision, you had better hope that perspective is the correct one. It is efficient to take a single approach, but if it's the wrong approach, you could efficiently go over a cliff. Rarely is this a good way to make decisions. In general, decision-making and problem-solving benefit from a broad search for information and a broad consideration of alternatives. A narrow focus works only when it is accurate or when it is the only one that matters.

The larger issue is that, when we follow the majority's way of thinking or its strategy to solve a problem, we are less likely to pay attention to other information or to a different problem that may arise. We are also less likely to use multiple strategies to solve the problem. This may be one reason for the tragedy of United Airlines Flight 173. There, a narrow focus led to more than inefficiency or a

near-miss—the plane literally fell out of the sky. Let's re-
visit that example in the light of this chapter.

> ▷ As you might recall from the introduction, United
> Airlines Flight 173 was en route from Denver to Port-
> land when the crew heard a noise and vibration. The
> light that normally indicated that the landing gear was
> down did not come on. The captain and crew all focused
> on finding the problem with the landing gear. What they
> did not notice or, more accurately, did not express was
> that they were running out of fuel. They crashed in a
> suburb of Portland only six nautical miles east/southeast
> of the airport.   ◁

Many people might think that one individual could be
so focused on the landing gear problem that he wouldn't
have noticed the fuel gauge—but three people? An experienced crew, including a captain, a first officer, and a flight
engineer? In general, we assume that, with more numbers,
a group is better able to solve problems, but in fact, if
those numbers form a consensus, they can be an impediment to solving the problem. Consensus also makes it less
likely that any one person will speak up even if he notices
another problem or has a different solution.

In the case of United Airlines Flight 173, the captain
did not give a clear order to focus only on the landing gear.
He was not a Jim Jones with surveillance over the crew's

focus. The power came from the consensus. For forty-five minutes, they focused narrowly on one problem (the landing gear) and gave scant attention to another emerging problem (low fuel). In effect, they were forming words using only a backward sequence of letters.

After this tragedy, people pointed to the silver lining of "lessons learned." The National Transportation Safety Board laid blame on both the captain and the crew members. In summary, the NTSB observed that the captain was preoccupied with the landing gear malfunction and didn't listen to the crew, but the crew members, for their part, didn't communicate the urgency of the situation. Consensus failed them.

The United Airlines incident points to another kind of following—following through silence, that is, not speaking up when we see a problem or note a deficiency. The crew was silent. They noticed the level of fuel. The Portland control tower even asked about it. The crew members may have spoken about it, but they did not "speak up." In their collective timidity, it was a cockpit variant of what happens when "good men do nothing."

The NTSB recognized that the crew may have conformed to the captain's "way of thinking." The investigators understood that the explanation for the crew's actions was not as simple as conformity or a willingness to follow orders. However, they did not recognize that the unanimity of the crew added to this way of thinking. All the research suggests that had someone spoken up, had the consensus been broken, the power of the consensus would have been diminished. The crew members would have been more likely to think for themselves.

The NTSB's preferred solution, like every university or organization that I know, was education and training in order to achieve "participative management" for captains and "assertiveness training" for crew members. In other words, the captain can't be king, effectively shutting down information and questions from his subordinates. The crew members have to speak up. Training is the "go to" solution in many organizations. It can be helpful. In general, however, it is not very effective in combating biases.

I would argue that training also is not very effective in getting people to speak up. There are realities to power and hierarchies. People don't give up power and position willingly, and speaking up has costs, real or imagined. We find it difficult to speak up when we are in the minority or when we think we lack sufficient expertise. We are helped when a rebel is present. The real peril of consensus is when it goes unchallenged.

We know that a narrow perspective impairs good decision-making. It also impairs original thinking. As an example of the closed mind fostered by consensus, one of our studies investigated the originality of thought as a product of exposure to a majority opinion. Participants judged the color of a series of blue slides. In one condition, they learned that most people (80 percent) saw these slides as green. In the control condition, they received no feedback as to others' judgments. They then completed a word association task. They simply gave seven word associations with the word "blue" and seven word associations with the word "green." The findings showed that those exposed to the majority judgment that blue slides were green gave more conventional associations and were less original than those in the control groups.

THE OTHER SIDE OF CONSENSUS AND FOCUS

This discussion would be incomplete if we left the impression that consensus and focused thought have only negative effects. In general, a focused perspective is detrimental to decision-making and problem-solving, but there are times when it provides advantages. A narrow focus is helpful when it's correct. It is certainly efficient. But even then, the narrow focus still limits the range of considerations and lessens the likelihood of seeing problems that may emerge.

In a study testing the potential advantages of consensus-driven thought, my colleagues and I found that the hard part was finding a task where a narrow perspective could be an advantage. We did find one, however; it is called the Stroop test. It is an unusual test in that performance depends on being able to focus on one dimension while ignoring another. In the task, a series of color words are printed in different colors of ink. The instructions are to read the colors of ink as quickly and accurately as possible.

You will have to use your imagination to understand this task, since this book is printed in black and white. Imagine being shown these words:

YELLOW WHITE BLUE RED

Now picture the word "YELLOW" printed in red ink, the word "WHITE" in green ink, the word "BLUE" in black ink, and the word "RED" in blue ink. You might want to write these words on a piece of paper to see the task more clearly.

Your job is to read the four words as "RED GREEN BLACK BLUE." These are the colors of ink. What you will find is that when you try to do this quickly, you start to say the color name you are reading ("YELLOW") rather than the ink color ("RED"). The reason is that this is a classic task of interference: the name of the color interferes with the color of the ink.

The Stroop test is one of the few tasks where focusing on one dimension of the stimulus word is advantageous. However, you have to focus on the right dimension (the ink) and be able to ignore the other dimension (the name). It is one of the few tasks where limiting information is beneficial. People have difficulty doing this on their own. Either they slow down a lot, to avoid saying the name, or they make a lot of errors. That's why the instructions are to do it as quickly and as accurately as you can.

In our study, the focus of a majority judgment was varied. In one condition, the majority focused on the name of the word; in another condition, they focused on the color of ink. In either case, the participants followed the focus of that majority. So those exposed to a majority who focused on the ink color also focused on ink and thus performed the Stroop test significantly better. They were faster and more accurate. Those exposed to a majority who focused on the name of the color (the wrong dimension) focused on name and performed far more poorly on the Stroop test. In either case, they took the majority perspective.

In one condition, the focus was right (ink), and in the other it was wrong (name). On the Stroop test, focus translated into being either an advantage or a disadvantage. On the test as elsewhere, a single focus, if it is the right one, can be efficient. The problem of course is that a single focus is rarely an advantage and we rarely know if the majority's focus is the right one. However, our study demonstrates that a narrow focus can in principle be an advantage if a task requires ignoring some information.

In sum, majority judgments, especially when they form a consensus, stimulate a narrow focus on the issue from the majority's perspective. This focus narrows the slice of information we seek, the options we consider, and the problem-solving strategies we employ. It acts as a filter, inducing us to think like the majority. While we are able to use the general principle to advantage or disadvantage, the general finding is that a narrow focus impedes the quality of our decision-making and problem-solving.

5 DISSENT DIVERSIFIES— AND STRENGTHENS THINKING

In Part I, we saw how majority and minority voices convince others to agree with their position. Those ways differed simply by virtue of whether the persuader was one of "the many" or one of "the few." We saw that majorities and minorities have different routes for gaining agreement and tend to change attitudes at different levels (for example, public versus private). In Part II, we have seen that the influence of majority and minority opinion is broader than simple efforts to persuade or gain agreement. Whether or not we come to agree with or follow those seeking influence over us, they change the way we think about the issue. The effect on our thinking is diametrically different, however, depending on whether influence is coming from a majority or minority viewpoint.

In the last chapter, we looked at the influence of the majority. Majorities, especially when they are unchallenged, influence us to think in narrow ways and in a biased manner, more so than we would without such influence. That bias has direction; in particular, we think from the majority perspective. So we select information that confirms the majority position and we use majority strategies in problem-solving. We become complicit in looking at the issue from the majority point of view—even if we show no agreement with the majority position. As a result, the quality of our decision-making and problem-solving often suffers.

In this chapter, we will see that dissenting opinion— the view of "the few"—also changes the way we think. But here the news is good. When exposed to a dissenting opinion, we think more divergently than we would on our own. We do this whether the dissent is right or wrong. To use a metaphor, we explore different routes. We seek information on all sides of the issue. We explore more diverse options. As a result, we are better able to make good decisions and detect novel solutions.

There are benefits to dissent. In Chapter 2, we saw that one benefit of dissent is that it breaks the power of the majority to achieve blind following. In this chapter, we will see even greater benefits of dissent. Dissent stimulates us to think in ways that are less biased, more open, and more divergent. If we had unlimited money and knowl-edge, most researchers would try to train people to think this way in order to raise the quality of judgment and decision-making. Training is often ineffective or has short-term effects, while here we have a robust mechanism that achieves such results. Dissent, then, is not just an antidote to consensus; more importantly, it stimulates our thinking so that we look at multiple sides of the issue, detect new solutions, and even think in more original ways.

The value of dissent does not depend on the heroism of the dissenter or the correctness of the dissenting position. We usually don't see the value of dissent—or we don't see it until later, if the dissenting position has been proven right, such as in the case of Galileo. What I will argue is that dissent has value even when it has not convinced us, and *even when it is wrong.* Its value lies in the thought that it stimulates in us. Far better than awareness or training designed to stimulate thinking, dissent prompts us to actually reconsider our positions and contemplate alternatives.

DISSENT AS LIBERATOR: A REFRESHER

In Chapter 2, we saw that dissent provides an antidote to the power of the majority to get us to agree with them, even when the dissenter is wrong and even when she is not an ally. Just one challenge is all it takes to break the power of consensus, because the power of the majority lies in its unanimity. Dissent breaks that unanimity, and one result is that it increases our independence.

In those early studies, we learned that many people agree with a majority that is wrong, even when their eyes tell them otherwise. Researchers tried to understand why this happens and wondered what could serve as an antidote. How do you get people to resist the majority and think for themselves? An antidote was already apparent in those early studies. Although they didn't call it "dissent," they found that any challenge to the majority breaks its power to get us to blindly follow.

Truth matters less than we might wish. We follow majorities, right or wrong. Dissent breaks that hold of the majority whether it is right or wrong and even if the dissenter has almost no credibility. Imagine if the dissenter in the Asch length-of-line studies had obviously poor vision. In an amusing study, Vern Allen and John Levine, who were then at the University of Wisconsin, looked at just that. Using visual stimuli like the length of lines as well as other items, they devised a study that had an ally walking into the study wearing thick glasses. He asked the experimenter whether the task involved long-distance sight, discussed his vision problems, and even failed an informal vision test. One can imagine that the participants were thinking that this person would be of no help in determining the length of lines. He obviously didn't see well.

Even though participants reported that this individual's vision was likely poor, his social support mattered. With him serving as a dissenter and an ally in the study, conformity dropped significantly. It was one-third lower than when no ally was present. What is important about these studies is that they show that unanimity is at the heart of the majority's power. When it is broken, people don't follow the majority to error. When that happens, we see the power of the one who stands up—even if he is wrong and even if his judgment is seriously in doubt. Dissent in almost any form breaks consensus and benefits our independence and our ability to think for ourselves. We "know what we know" and are more willing to express it.

We now turn to the second and perhaps more important benefit.

DISSENT AS A STIMULATOR OF THOUGHT

The main topic of this chapter—and the second benefit of dissent—is that it stimulates divergent thinking. Exposed to dissent, we become more open, more curious, and more likely to consider multiple perspectives. We even become more original in our thinking. Before embarking on the experimental evidence to support this contention, let me take you on a personal journey to explain how these ideas originated. It may feel familiar to you. This is perhaps the most personal section of this book. The power of dissent is the topic that has preoccupied me for decades, and it has become a way of thinking for me, even the basis for deeply held values.

My serious study of the potential benefits of dissent did not come from an event in my youth, nor did it come from a specific occurrence, like a faculty meeting or a news story. I wasn't that smart. It came to me in the course of doing research on the requirement of unanimity in juries.

Contrary to what many believe, not all American juries are required to deliberate to unanimity. Oregon and Louisiana do not require unanimity, and several defendants who were convicted by 10–2 or 11–1 verdicts later appealed their verdicts based on due process and equal protection under the law. Had they been judged in Missouri, for example, the jury would have had to be unanimous. The US Supreme Court in 1972 disagreed with their arguments for appeal of their convictions and ruled that the defendants' constitutional rights had not been violated. Their guilty verdicts were upheld.

While a professor at the University of Virginia, I studied this issue. My first lines of inquiry were conventional for the times. Much as in the research covered in Part I, my students and I studied who "won"—namely, whether the votes and verdicts changed if unanimity rather than some form of majority rule was required. We conducted our research in both an experimental study and an actual courtroom, in collaboration with the University of Virginia Law School. To track the deliberations, we coded every comment—who made it, to whom it was addressed, and the nature of the comment. There was one about every four seconds. Together with the greatest group of four undergraduates you can imagine, I spent hundreds of hours watching these tapes—over and over and over.

We published these studies, but the real insight came from repeatedly watching those tapes. When unanimity was required, the dissenters seemed to argue more vigorously and over a longer period of time. What became clear to me was that this improved the quality of the discussion and the decision-making process. The participants considered more evidence and more ways of explaining that evidence. Instead of rushing to judgment, they considered alternatives. They discussed various possibilities for the same set of facts. *Was the presence of pills and alcohol evidence for suicide? Or could it indicate an accidental overdose? Or perhaps it was murder?* This is the kind of thinking that we saw when there was a persistent dissenter. This is divergent thinking.

That insight took hold and led to a research program that lasted for decades. My early work was geared to testing cause and effect. Does dissent stimulate divergent thinking, or do they co-occur for other reasons? Is the nature of thought different without dissent? My later work concentrated on the quality of decisions and the creativity of solutions. Consistently, we found that dissent opens the mind and stimulates divergent thinking, the kind of thinking that is wide and curious as well as deep and scrutinizing.

This chapter, in many ways, is the mirror image of Chapter 4. We will review many of the same studies, since they compared the thinking stimulated by consensus with that stimulated by dissent, and both were compared to control conditions. In Chapter 4, we compared consensus to control conditions and repeatedly found that consensus focuses and narrows the mind to the perspective of the consensus. Here we compare dissent to those control conditions and will see the diametrically opposite results. Dissent opens the mind and widens the range of considerations.

The Search for Information—Pros and Cons

As a rule, we are not generally open to information that opposes our beliefs, especially when we are convinced that we are right. We favor information that confirms our own beliefs. When we face consensus that disagrees with our position, however, we do the opposite of what we would do normally. In a powerful twist, rather than look for support for our own position, we prefer information that confirms the consensus. We don't look at both sides. We take the consensus perspective rather than our own and primarily seek information that supports the consensus position.

In the presence of dissent, we don't narrow our search to any one position, whether our own or that of the dissenter. Instead, we expand and widen our search. We seek information on both sides of the issue and consider the cons as well as the pros of positions, including our own.

In a study, which we described in Chapter 4, university students were given the results of a survey on proposals they strongly opposed. They were then provided an opportunity to read information favoring or opposing the proposals. The results showed that the information they chose to read was strongly affected by the percentage of students who took the opposite stance, that is, who favored these dreaded proposals. When a large majority favored the proposals, participants wanted to read information that could explain and confirm the majority position. When only a minority of students favored the proposals—that is, when there was a dissenting position—the search for information was quite different.

When participants learned that a minority of individuals favored the dreaded proposals, they wanted more information in general. They wanted to read more articles as well as longer articles, and their search for information was greater than in any other condition. Of particular importance, they wanted to see the reasons for *both* viewpoints. There was no evidence of bias in their choice of information to read. They chose approximately the same number of articles favoring the proposals as opposing them. They were as interested in learning the reasons why people favored the proposals as they were in learning the reasons why people opposed the proposals. They wanted to read information that supported their own position as well as information that opposed their position. These results held whether or not the proposals affected them personally—that is, whether the proposals would be implemented while they were still students or years later.

Attending Widely and Detecting New Solutions

The finding that dissenting views stimulate divergent thinking in the search for information is paralleled in other studies. In one, this involved recall of information. When individuals faced dissent, they had better memory for informational details. The procedure was as follows:

Participants in groups of four heard a tape recording of fourteen words. They were asked to name the category of word they first noticed. Of the fourteen words, four were types of fruit, and there were two words each from the categories of birds, furniture, tools, clothing, and transportation. On their own, participants first noticed the category of fruits. It was the category with the most words out of the fourteen, plus the first and last words on the list were from this category. There were three such lists comprising fourteen words each.

In one set of conditions, participants learned that one person in their four-person group first noticed a different category—birds. Everyone else first noticed the fruit category. It was a very simple manipulation. This occurred on either the first list only or on all three lists. After this feedback, the participants heard a recording of all forty-two words from the three lists, but in random order. After listening to the recording, they then wrote down every word they could remember. Following this, they heard a list of thirty completely new words from still different categories and then wrote down every word they could remember.

Compared to a control group who received no information about what anyone had first noticed, those who had learned of a dissenting position remembered more words. They remembered both more of the original forty-two words and more words from the new list of thirty words involving completely different categories. They paid better attention to the information.

Consistency over time was again revealed as important for the power of dissent. It was the repeated noticing of the bird category on all three lists, rather than on just one, that stimulated this significant improvement in recall. Much like the research on persuasion discussed in Chapter 3, dissent needs consistency to have impact. That is, to spark this curious and divergent way of thinking, it is more effective to not only express your counterposition but to do so more than once, to do so consistently and persistently over time.

Adding to the evidence that dissent stimulates attention to a wide variety of information is a third study. This one, briefly described in Chapter 4, involves the detection of embedded figures. By stimulating a more careful perusal of the stimuli, dissent helped participants to detect new solutions. In this study, participants were asked to find all the comparison figures where a hanging man image was embedded. It was a simple version of *Where's Waldo*. You may remember that when a majority noticed the image somewhere other than the obvious, the participants followed them exactly, right or wrong. They did not appear to even look at alternative possibilities, and they failed to find other correct solutions. By contrast, when it was a minority who noticed the image elsewhere, people did not follow them—but they did find the correct solutions in the other comparison figures. They looked carefully at all the comparison figures. They also were not just guessing: they found significantly more correct solutions than did people in the control condition or people who faced a majority.

Dissent benefited the detection of correct solutions, even ones not suggested by the dissenters.

Utilizing Multiple Strategies

The consequences of dissent for opening the mind are greater than the breadth of the information we seek or remember and greater than even our attention to the multiple facets of the situation. Dissent also promotes better problem-solving by stimulating the usage of multiple strategies or routes to solutions. As discussed earlier, when we solve a problem in multiple ways, we often find more and better solutions, and we are more likely to detect our errors. Dissent stimulates our use of a wide array of strategies, to our benefit.

To illustrate, reconsider another study briefly described in the last chapter—the one in which individuals in groups of four were shown a letter string—for example, "rTAPe." They named the first word they noticed, which was the word in capital letters reading from left to right—TAP in this example. When given feedback as to what the other four in their group first saw, the conditions differed. Either a majority (of three) or a minority (of one) repeatedly named the word formed by the backward sequencing of the capital letters—PAT.

We saw in Chapter 4 that, when the majority did this, participants used primarily one strategy to see words in the letter string—the backward sequencing of letters, as used by the majority. This changed when it was a single individual—a dissenter—who consistently saw the word formed by backward sequencing. In this condition, the participants opened their minds and used all available strategies. They didn't just follow the dissenter's one strategy of backward sequencing but formed words using all three strategies: forward, backward, and mixed sequencing of letters. They didn't just see "par and ear"; they also saw "rap and art." They also performed at a higher level. By using all strategies, they formed significantly more words than in any other condition.

TWO EXEMPLARS: A FILM AND A REAL-LIFE CASE

The most important takeaway from this book is the idea that dissent stimulates us to think divergently—to seek information and consider options in multiple directions, to use more strategies, to be more open than we would be on our own. As a result, dissent leads to improved performance and better decision-making in groups, findings that will be more fully documented in Part III but which are well illustrated in the film *Twelve Angry Men*.

In Chapter 3, we discussed how that film shows the ways in which the dissenting position can prevail. Henry Fonda's character, the lone vote for a "not guilty" verdict, persuades the other eleven jurors to agree with him, and the film illustrates some of the subtlety of how he achieved that. The film also depicts an even more important benefit of dissent—its stimulation of divergent thinking and its value for the quality of the decision-making.

As the film opens, the eleven jurors who favor a "guilty" verdict see no reason for discussion—it is an open-and-shut case of first-degree murder. We might have expected them to rush to judgment, pummel the dissenter into submission, and render a verdict of "guilty." Yet they do not, thanks to the dissent of Fonda's character.

To recap, the evidence looks overwhelming. There were two eyewitnesses. One was an elderly man who lived downstairs from the crime scene. He testified that he heard a fight, and specifically that he heard "the kid" (the defendant) say to his father, "I'm going to kill you"; then the elderly man heard the body hit the floor. He ran to the door and saw the defendant coming down the stairs, so he called the police. On arrival, the police found the father with a knife in his chest. These are "facts," according to the juror played by Lee J. Cobb. There is nothing to discuss. Yet, after consistent and persistent dissent by Fonda and his repeated question, "But couldn't they be wrong?" the jurors start to show divergent thinking.

They ask for a diagram of the apartments, look at the room measurements, and reenact the elderly witness's testimony. Role-playing his account allows them to come to an agreement on the amount of time that would have lapsed between hearing the body hit the floor and running to the door to see the defendant coming down the stairs. They discover that the elderly witness couldn't have reached the door in that short a time. They also take into account the loud noise of the passing train, which would have made it unlikely that anyone could hear the sound of a body hitting the floor with any accuracy. This raises doubt about this witness's testimony. Fonda's dissent has stimulated the jurors to search for more information (the diagram), use more strategies to assess the accuracy of the testimony (reenactment), notice other potentially pertinent facts (the roar of the train), and consider alternatives, such as possible motives or misperceptions on the part of the eyewitness.

In real life, pure examples of the power of dissent are harder to find than film dramatizations because events in real life usually occur for multiple reasons and have multiple consequences. However, the example of Edward Snowden seems a good vehicle for demonstrating the operation of some of these principles. In leaking documents related to National Security Agency surveillance, he spoke with a minority voice. He challenged authority, but he also challenged a populace that was trusting of government surveillance. Snowden's dissent was not in leaking documents; that was the vehicle. His dissent was in challenging the majority's beliefs and complacency about the government being benign when it came to the collection of personal information. His dissent was focused not only on exposing government practices but also on arguing for privacy. Snowden's position was that the surveillance system's practices were a breach of constitutional rights. In Chapter 2, we covered his ability to persuade—to change minds. Here we concentrate on the divergent thinking that his dissent stimulated.

▶ Edward Snowden was a minority of one. When he released the classified documents about the NSA surveillance system in May 2013, he was almost universally reviled. The press and the government came down hard on him. So did the politicians and self-proclaimed experts who saw him as a traitor. For them, he was someone who had leaked classified documents and endangered national security.

In many situations like this one, it is difficult to see the influence of dissent except for some indications from polls, surveys, or actual changes to the surveillance system. In Snowden's case, there was some evidence that he changed minds about the NSA surveillance system, but even that took time. More importantly, the Snowden case is illustrative of a broader kind of influence depicted in this chapter. Snowden sparked a change in the way we thought about this issue as well as other issues. One example is President Obama's State of the Union speech in January 2014.

President Obama, who had vigorously defended the surveillance program, revealed in this speech that he had pivoted to a broader set of considerations. He had changed from defender-in-chief to someone who was thoughtful about the various ways to view the issue. In the seven months since the Snowden leaks, he had consulted with everyone—oversight boards, foreign partners, industry leaders, even skeptics—in a divergent search for information. In his speech, the president skillfully summarized the opposing positions. He understood the difficulties in having efficient intelligence gathering while also protecting privacy rights. He understood the fallout for commercial ventures, for relations with other governments, and for the trust of the American people. Friend and foe alike praised his ability to take into account multiple interests and perspectives. Using our terms here, President Obama had gone from convergent thinking in defending the system to more divergent thinking in considering the rationale for various positions. He recognized that this was not just an issue of illegal leaking of classified information; there were broader considerations of surveillance and privacy, which extended to business, foreign policy, and domestic trust. ◄

There was other evidence of divergent thinking after the Snowden leaks. Ordinary people were searching for new information and pondering many issues through the lens of privacy. Before, we might have thought about drones in terms of their ability to deliver packages or to help firefighters or realtors. Now we also saw the possibility for drones invading our airspace and disrupting our peace and quiet. Before, we might have clicked on "Agree" to the terms of a website without reflecting on the fact that we were giving permission to the wholesale tracking and usage of our personal data. Now we had become more concerned about the storage and use of our data. Many of us revisited history, from the founding fathers to the Church Committee, which had warned us of the dangers of surveillance and intelligence abuses during the Vietnam War era.

After the Snowden leaks, I myself went to see the documentary *Terms and Conditions May Apply* in a small cinema in the Mission District of San Francisco and had heated discussions with people in cafés, including a founder of the enterprise unit of Google. We discussed the pros and cons of drones, "Big Brother" surveillance, and privacy in this Internet age. I can guarantee you that I wouldn't have made these observations or had these discussions—and I certainly would not have gone to that small theater—if not for the thinking sparked by Edward Snowden's dissent. We all were thinking in divergent ways. Our thinking became broader and even more scrutinizing.

Real-life stories are multiply determined. There are undoubtedly many reasons why people began searching broadly for information on both privacy and national security after 2013. One of those reasons, however, was most likely Edward Snowden's views and behavior. As the research shows, dissent stimulates a search for information on both sides of an issue, and the thinking that ensues can then extend to other situations.

MOVING BETWEEN STRATEGIES AND CREATIVITY

Sometimes we need more than just an open mind to widen and deepen our thinking. We need to integrate the various ways of thinking and options. We need to move flexibly from one focus to another. Being able to do so brings us closer to creativity and creative solutions, or at least to greater flexibility of thought. This appears to be another benefit of dissent: it enables us not only to see different paths but to shift from one path to another as needed.

If you remember the Stroop test described in Chapter 4, you will recall that it is one of the few tasks where convergent (not divergent) thinking is an advantage—*if* the focus is on the right dimension. If you are executing what is a good idea and you are on the right path, convergent thinking gives you an advantage much like wearing blinders and moving efficiently.

In the study using the Stroop test, we saw that a majority stimulated convergent thinking from the majority perspective. When the participants' focus was right—when they focused not on the color name but on the color of the ink in which the name was written—they performed better on the Stroop test. They focused on the ink and were able to ignore the distracting information about the name of the word. When their focus was wrong—when they focused on the color name and not on the color of the ink—they did more poorly. They again converged their thinking, but now it was on the wrong dimension—the color name—and they were unable to respond accurately with the ink color.

In a different but related study, a former graduate student and I investigated the ability of an individual to move flexibly from one focus to another. Could participants move from a focus on ink to a focus on name as appropriate? Here we find that it is the dissenter who stimulates this flexibility. Following the theory up to now, you might expect that people exposed to dissent would focus on both the ink and the name, a form of divergent thinking. Yet the Stroop test is difficult precisely because we see colors in both the ink and name, so it is hard to ignore one of them. What you might not expect is that dissent does more than stimulate a consideration of both dimensions. It provides us with the flexibility to use the one that is most appropriate.

This new study followed a procedure similar to that of the earlier one. Here, we studied the influence of the minority voice, the dissenter, who focused in the initial phase on *either* the ink or the name. Let me try to describe this so you can visualize it.

If participants are shown a slide with two words, one being the word "BLUE" in blue ink, for example, and the other being a word such as "YELLOW" in green ink, they will tend to say that "BLUE" is the first color they notice, since the color of the ink and the name are the same. In this study, one person, our dissenter, consistently chose a different word. That choice indicated that she was focused either on the ink (if she said "green") or on the name (if she said "yellow"). That simple manipulation established that the dissenter was in the minority and indicated the dimension on which she focused. We wanted to test the ability of the participants to shift from one focus to the other, depending on what was most appropriate. Here is how we tested that flexibility.

Instead of reading only the color of ink, as required by the Stroop task, the participants were asked to shift from ink to name. In the "high-flexibility" condition, they had to shift their focus every third word. It was not easy to go from calling out the ink color to calling out the name color every three answers. In the "low-flexibility" condition, they shifted from calling out the ink color to calling out the name color, but one page at a time—for one page of words, they were to focus on the ink color, and on the next page they were to focus on the name color. In this "low-flexibility" condition, participants did not have to continuously shift back and forth.

The results showed that it didn't matter whether the minority focused on the ink or on the name. Their particular position didn't matter. What mattered was that they were a minority voice. Participants didn't follow them, but were able to consider both dimensions. It was divergent, but it was also more flexible. Importantly for this task, participants were better able to shift from reading the ink color to reading the name color, as appropriate.

This flexibility of thought in the Stroop test was mainly evident in the high-flexibility condition. It was when participants had to rapidly shift back and forth between dimensions that the value of dissent was most evident. Dissent aided the participants' ability to shift every third word, using the appropriate dimension. Their performance time was better than in any other condition. The important point from this study is that we learn something more important from dissent than the specific position taken by the dissenter. We become better able to consider multiple positions and to shift from one to another as appropriate. As our thinking becomes more flexible, we develop a looseness of thought, one which we will see benefits creativity.

This element of flexibility and the ability to shift between various points of view may be especially important in complex decision-making. It is one thing to consider various options in sequence, but another to move flexibly between them. One real-life application in the medical world illustrates the importance of seeking out differing views, even dissent, for flexibility of thinking.

Really good doctors show flexibility in moving from one strategy to another. They invite differences of opinion from different specialists, and then move flexibly between those perspectives to diagnose a set of symptoms. Jacob Johnson, one of the best ENT physicians in the San Francisco Bay Area, knows a great deal about ears, noses, and throats. But in medically complicated situations, he invites opinions from pulmonologists, sleep specialists, and even dentists and surgeons from other fields who have pertinent knowledge. He then moves from one set of information and opinion to the next in his search for solutions.

In one case, Dr. Johnson was faced with a patient who had a complicated set of symptoms, including sleep apnea. Consulting the various specialists, he moved flexibly from pulmonologists to sleep specialists to those trained in the most recent techniques before deciding that a sleep-induced endoscopy would give him a more complete picture of the patient's condition. This kind of endoscopy is an exquisitely fine-tuned technique that would help him see how, and possibly why, the throat was closing when the patient was going to sleep. As it turned out, the specialist in that procedure was leaving the area permanently. Dr. Johnson was not discouraged. He had the requisite skills himself and, just as importantly, had become adept at flexible thinking, so he brought together a skilled and experienced team and did the procedure himself. The information that he gleaned from performing the procedure and from consultations with specialists were integrated and became part of a more complete picture and diagnosis, culminating in the avoidance of surgery and the usage of forms of therapy.

A NOTE ABOUT CREATIVITY
AND DISSENT—AND BRAINSTORMING

Most definitions of creativity include the elements of originality and appropriateness to a solution. Originality is related to the uniqueness of ideas, though sometimes it is the combination of ideas that is original. Appropriateness is important because not just any crazy idea can be considered creative. A creative idea is one that addresses a problem. It turns out that consensus and dissent affect originality directly and in opposite directions. We saw in Chapter 4 that consensus stimulates conventional thinking and lowers originality. We will now see that dissent stimulates originality of thought.

The study used an old method, one popularized by Sigmund Freud: word associations. In that study, we looked at the originality of word associations as a product of being exposed to a majority or minority opinion that differed from their own. These were compared to a control condition where they had no such exposure. To remind you of the procedure, we simply had participants judge the color of a series of blue slides. In one condition, they received no feedback about how others judged these slides. In a second condition, they learned that most people (80 percent) saw these slides as green. In a third condition, they learned that a minority of individuals (20 percent) saw the slides as green. They were then given the word association task. They gave a series of seven associations to the word "blue" and seven associations to the word "green."

In the previous chapter, we found that, when participants had faced an erroneous *majority* judgment that blue slides were green, they were significantly less original than when they did not have that experience. They stuck with highly common word associations and thus thought in a conventional manner. However, in the condition where they faced an erroneous *minority* judgment that blue slides were green, their word associations became significantly more original. Let's consider some examples.

Suppose I ask you for associations to the word "blue." What comes to mind? People normally start out with rather conventional associations such as "sky" and then move to more original associations, such as "jeans" or "jazz." For associations to the word "green," they may start out with a word like "grass" and move to a more original association such as "envy" or "back" (as in "greenback").

We were able to calculate the originality of their associations with these words because, luckily, data on people's associations with a whole host of words—including the words "blue" and "green"—are available. We were able to calculate the statistical likelihood of a given association. It is highly likely, for example, that someone will say "sky" as the first thing that comes to mind when I say "blue." It is far less likely that she will say "jeans." In this study, those facing the minority opinion, even when it was wrong, had more unique associations. Their associations were more original than those of a control group and certainly more original than the associations of those in the majority condition.

Originality is but one aspect of creative thought. Another and perhaps more important one is divergent thinking—the type of thinking that dissent stimulates. In fact, a common test for creativity is really a measure of divergent thinking. To illustrate, suppose I ask you to give me a number of uses for a brick, and you give me four: "to build a road," "to build a house," "to build a factory," and "to build an outhouse." But suppose you were to say instead: "to build a house," "to use as a doorstop," "to use as a missile," and "to use as a saucer." Again, you have given me four uses for a brick. However, the first set of four uses come from a single category of thinking: things that can be built with a brick. The second set of four uses of a brick includes not just building, but use as a missile, a doorstop, and a saucer. This greater range of categories of uses is more divergent. It is also more creative. This is actually a test for creativity.

The fact that dissent increases originality and divergent thinking led us to reconsider the rules of a popular technique for generating creative ideas, namely brainstorming. Usual practice and the advice of researchers as well as consultants tends to argue against disagreement, debate, and criticism of ideas.

From the inception of brainstorming by Alex Osborn in the 1950s until quite recently, there have been rules for brainstorming. These are rules that are assumed to benefit idea generation but which, by and large, have gone unexamined. People have argued over whether brainstorming is effective or not, but there has been little attempt to examine the four rules. Those rules are: (1) emphasize quantity of ideas; (2) build on the ideas of others; (3) engage in freewheeling; and, especially, (4) do not criticize. Most of these rules are intuitively plausible—for example, the rule about not criticizing the ideas of others. The assumption is that people will shut down if there is criticism of their ideas. A study we conducted in both the United States and France refutes this.

In a study of this important rule in the year 2000, we challenged the notion that criticism or debate would decrease the generation of ideas. In fact, we thought it possible that the number of ideas would *increase* with permission to criticize ideas. We did this study the hard way—by conducting it in two countries, the United States and France.

The study was fairly simple. Individuals in small groups brainstormed ideas to solve the problem of traffic congestion. This is a problem both in San Francisco and in Paris, where the studies were conducted. Participants were asked to come up with as many solutions to the problem as they could.

In two experimental conditions, they were given four rules. In a control condition, they were given no rules. The two experimental conditions differed in one simple respect: participants were either asked not to criticize each other (the traditional rule) or told to feel free to debate and even to criticize each other's ideas. The other three rules remained the same in both conditions and were the other rules of brainstorming originally posited by Osborn—freewheel, build on others' ideas, and emphasize quantity of ideas.

Most researchers would have predicted that encouraging debate, even criticism, would lead to fewer ideas than any other condition. They would predict that it would depress the number of ideas generated compared to the control condition where no rules were offered. They would also predict that the usual rule "do not criticize" would result in the most ideas. It should lead to more ideas than the control condition and certainly more ideas than encouragement to debate and even criticize the ideas of one another. In fact, we found otherwise. Allowing debate and criticism led to significantly more, not fewer, ideas than the control condition. And there was a trend in the direction of more ideas, not fewer, when debate and criticism were advised than when the groups were told "not to criticize." These results were found in both the United States and France.

For those of you interested in brainstorming, there is thoughtful research on the topic. However, the sacred rule of brainstorming—the rule not to criticize the ideas of others—is now in question. Our results were surprising to many, partly because the rule "do not criticize" was intuitively plausible and went unexamined. It also fits with the prevailing notion that harmony is the route to creativity in groups. In fact, the results suggest that the rule "do not criticize" may be less effective than permitting or encouraging criticism of ideas. The popular press is now considering how criticism can be utilized to enhance the value of brainstorming.

Criticism is not the same as dissent, but both point to the value of challenge for the generation of creative ideas. The idea here is that, rather than constrain ourselves by contemplating how not to offend or criticize, we should be free to truly brainstorm ideas. This might involve criticism of an idea. It is not a mandate to criticize, but rather permission to criticize. As with the advice regarding dissent, challenge is best when permitted, not fabricated— and even welcomed when it is authentic. As we will see in Chapter 7, authenticity is the key to the benefits of dissent.

Repeatedly we find that dissent has value, even when it is wrong, even when we don't like the dissenter, and even when we are not convinced of his position. Dissent breaks the hold of consensus and majority opinion and enables us to think more independently. Dissent also stimulates thought that is open, divergent, flexible, and original.

There are many important benefits to conflicting views; it even aids the brainstorming process itself.

I believe that part of the reason dissent opens the mind is that it makes us question our positions. Faced with an alternative conception of reality and a different way of thinking, we are brought closer to the kind of thinking we do when we are developing a position rather than defending or changing one. We actually search for and consider more options. This is of especially great benefit when groups are making decisions. This is the subject matter of the next section.

PART III

GROUPTHINK VERSUS GROUPS OF THINKERS

UP TO NOW, WE HAVE SEEN THAT THE SIMPLE FACT OF AN OPINION BEING either in the majority or in the minority has very different effects on people. When it is a majority, we take their perspective. We narrow the information we seek and how we approach a problem. Dissent, on the other hand, is one of the most powerful forms of influence for the liberation of thought. When faced with a minority opinion, we search for information and look at problems from multiple points of view—not just the minority's point of view, and not just our own. On balance, we make better judgments and are better able to detect new solutions. We even think in more original ways.

In Part III, we will explore these processes of consensus and dissent and their impact on decision-making in ongoing groups and organizations. It is one thing to manipulate consensus or dissent in experiments, as we did in Chapters 4 and 5, to see their effect on specific thought patterns. It is another thing to see these phenomena operate in real groups.

In Chapter 6, we will see why consensus, especially if it occurs early, is a problem for the quality of the discussion and for the quality of the decision. This is not just a problem when most everyone is in agreement at the outset. Groups move to consensus on their own via reliable and well-researched phenomena. Some of this movement is motivated, but much of it lies in the nature of the discourse. What is said and by whom is neither random nor equal; there are reliable patterns. Most of these processes move the group to consensus around the initial majority position; some make the judgment and decision more extreme than might have been predicted from the original individual positions.

In Chapter 7, we will address two presumed "antidotes" for this rush to consensus and, with it, poor decision-making processes: diversity and techniques such as devil's advocate. Supporters believe that these "antidotes" thwart pressure to consensus and lead to more divergent thinking. The problem is that, like most quick fixes, they don't work—at least not in the simple fashion in which they are promoted.

Diversity has "two heads" and can be an impediment as well as a benefit. One problem is that most people think of diversity in terms of categories—for example, gender or race—whereas, in fact, it is diversity of opinion that better predicts improved performance. And more than just a diversity of opinion, it is combat between different positions that provides the benefits for decision making. Devil's advocate is one of many techniques that try to create "pretend dissent": to plant an opposing view on the assumption that it will cause people to consider alternatives, to ponder the cons as well as the pros of their position. But as research has shown, it doesn't. We will see that such techniques do not clone the positive effects of authentic dissent. The stimulation for divergent thinking comes from the challenge posed by a dissenter who actually believes a different position—and is willing to say so.

6 GROUP DECISIONS: OFTEN IN ERROR, NEVER IN DOUBT

GROUPS OFTEN OPERATE IN A WAY THAT "STRAINS" FOR consensus, a term that Irving Janis, then at Yale, used to describe "groupthink." As his description of some major political fiascoes shows, such strain has been behind some truly poor decisions. One of the best-known decision fiascoes was the ill-fated US-backed invasion of Cuba at the Bay of Pigs in 1961. That decision has long been a staple of academic research into the failings of groups and is still enormously illuminating, especially through the lens of consensus and dissent. The Bay of Pigs decision-making was prototypical of groupthink and of Janis's model of bad decision-making.

"Straining for consensus" is basically the definition of "groupthink." The term has been used loosely in many settings. Some use it to refer to a "group mind," or to thinking "in concert." It is the core concept for understanding why truly bad decisions are made, and it is the centerpiece of Janis's ambitious model for how groups make decisions. Groupthink, in his words, is "the mode of thinking . . . when concurrence-seeking becomes so dominant . . . that it tends to override realistic appraisal of alternative courses of action."

Janis popularized the term in his book *Victims of Groupthink*, where he applied his model of group decision-making specifically to how some bad foreign policy decisions have been made. Janis's approach was inductive. He looked for patterns and commonalities among major political decision-making fiascoes by studying them in-depth, much like case studies. Unlike experiments that test hypotheses, he developed hypotheses from the similarities in these failed decisions. In so doing, he developed a model combining the antecedents, symptoms, and consequences of his core concept "groupthink."

The antecedents of this strain for consensus include cohesion, a directed leader, high stress, and little optimism within the group for a solution better than the leader's preferred position. Various symptoms of groupthink then emerge, such as stereotyping of out-groups, the illusion of invulnerability, self-censorship, the illusion of unanimity, and direct pressure on dissenters. And perhaps most important, the consequences of these symptoms are the elements of bad decision-making: an incomplete survey of alternatives and objectives, poor information search, selective bias, and a failure to examine the risk of the preferred choice. These are all examples of what we have called "convergent thinking" in prior chapters. The Bay of Pigs incident is a good example.

▶ Ever since Fidel Castro overthrew General Fulgencio Batista and took over Cuba in 1959, relations with the United States had been poor—so much so that in the early 1960s there was US interest in overthrowing his regime. Those who had fled Cuba were willing to fight for that cause. President Dwight D. Eisenhower had approved a plan in 1960 to train these exiles, and the new president, John F. Kennedy, was presented with it. In 1961, the decision was made to use CIA-trained Cuban exiles to invade Cuba. They did so on April 17, 1961.

The chronology of that invasion would be comical had its consequences not been so serious. The invasion force "immediately came under heavy fire. Cuban planes strafed the invaders, sank two escort ships, and destroyed half of the exile's air support." The Cuban exiles were surrounded and captured almost immediately. In the aftermath, the US government was publicly embarrassed, Cuba and the Soviet Union became more closely aligned, and relations between the United States and Castro's

Cuba became even more strained. More than fifty years later, we are only now making preliminary attempts to normalize relations.

Reportedly, Kennedy said at the time, "How could I have been so stupid as to let them proceed?"

It's clear that it wasn't a lack of intelligence on his part or that of the decision-making group, which included the secretaries of State and Defense, the Joint Chiefs of Staff, the CIA director, and a few eminent and trusted Harvard academics. The group was highly intelligent, but it does not take stupid people to make stupid decisions.

According to the groupthink model, one antecedent of the strain for consensus is a highly cohesive yet insulated group. The cabinet-level decision-making group that made the Bay of Pigs decision was such a group. They were highly cohesive—they stuck together and were unified—and they met in isolation. Another antecedent is a "directed leader" who lets you know his preferred position practically from the outset. In the Bay of Pigs decision, President Kennedy favored the invasion and everyone knew it. In fact, subsequent research has shown inconsistent results for cohesion being an antecedent of groupthink, but there is good evidence for the importance of the directed leader. Having a leader state a preference at the outset fosters a groupthink set of symptoms.

In the groupthink model, common symptoms of bad decision-making in groups—ones to watch out for—are rationalization and hubris. Members have an illusion of invulnerability, a belief in their own inherent morality, and they stereotype the outgroup or the enemy. These symptoms are an un-ironic version of Garrison Keillor's description of the fictional Lake Wobegon as the place where "the women are strong and the men good-looking, and all the children above average." Believing they were bigger, stronger, and smarter than the adversary, the Kennedy team grossly overestimated the Cubans' willingness to overthrow Castro and grossly underestimated the Cuban military. The Bay of Pigs decision was characterized by a biased information search, inadequate consideration of the alternatives to invasion, and a failure to examine the risks of an invasion. In fact, the president and his advisers were so sure of their easy success that they didn't even develop reasonable contingency plans. Given the swampy conditions, planning an escape route over many miles of marshland was hardly reasonable.

The other symptoms of groupthink are more important from the point of view of this book. They can be summarized as shutting down dissent. One way is by direct pressure on dissenters. Another is self-censorship. Both are facilitated by self-appointed mind guards.

Bobby Kennedy was one of those mind guards. He put pressure on those who seemed to have doubts. For example, he knew that Arthur Schlesinger opposed the invasion plan, so he took Schlesinger aside at a large birthday party and asked him why he was not in favor of it. After listening, Bobby Kennedy said, "You may be right or you may be wrong, but the President has made his mind up. Don't push it any further. Now is the time for everyone to help him all they can." Schlesinger later regretted censoring himself. "I bitterly reproached myself for having kept so silent during those crucial discussions in the cabinet room."

Many people would agree that the poor decision-making that went into the Bay of Pigs invasion was due to the "development of group norms that bolster morale at the expense of critical thinking." This dynamic obviously contributed to the consensus among the president's advisers, but does not provide a complete picture. Neither does a single descriptive phrase like "strain for consensus."

Janis's model is descriptive. It shows what he considered to be the antecedents, the symptoms during group discussion, and the elements of poor decision-making in a group. However, his model is also meant to be predictive. He theorized that these antecedents and symptoms "caused" the elements of bad decision-making. The problem is that there has been little research on the model, and what little there is has shown mixed results for the model as a whole. As mentioned earlier, however, the research does seem to support the notion that a directed leader, one who makes his preference known at the outset, sets in motion a myriad of decision-making processes that end in bad decisions.

Even if the causal relations are not well established, Janis put his finger on a central problem in these groups which made bad decisions. It was the emphasis on morale rather than critical thinking. This was shown by norms that group members agree and that they show loyalty by backing the group—no matter if they had reservations. In other words, the central problem lies in the norms that foster consensus and suppress dissent.

What will be familiar to you after reading Part II is that the pressure to reach consensus and especially the suppression of dissent are precisely the ways to get convergent thinking—a narrowing of the range of information and options by viewing the issue from a single perspective instead of exploring multiple perspectives. This is evident in the description of groups like the Bay of Pigs team. Their poor decision-making involved a biased information search, an inadequate consideration of alternatives, a failure to examine the risk of the preferred choice, and a failure to develop a reasonable contingency plan—precisely the ways of thinking that we have discussed as part of convergent thinking.

All the ways in which groups promote consensus and discourage dissent become part of the problem. Our desire to foster agreement, put pressure on dissent, and self-censor doesn't just come automatically from cohesion or even a directed leader, nor does it come from a simple preference for agreement or from individual motivations. A large part of this comes from normal group processes that prevail in everyday life just as they do in dramatic foreign policy decisions. These common processes contribute to a group's narrow focus, premature consensus, and exaggerated positions. It is common for groups to favor the initial preference and rush confidently to judgment. More often, it parallels convergent thinking, which, as we will see, is often exacerbated in groups.

GROUPS AND CONSENSUS

Group processes, by and large, conspire to suppress the very diversity of viewpoints that we seek. As we interact with others, we start to develop a shared view of an issue. Whatever differences we have in the beginning become fewer. It is not just that we want to conform or to agree with the majority opinion. It is that the group interaction itself has particular patterns that conspire to limit the range of information considered by the group. It is our desire to seek agreement, coupled with some common group processes, that contributes to poor decisions. A group doesn't need a directed leader, and it doesn't need cohesion or high stress. By their nature, groups move in the direction of consensus.

There are several ways in which groups make us more like one another, more uniform in our opinions, and more prone to making faulty group decisions. What all groups have in common is that they either start with relative homogeneity of opinion or they manage to create it. The consensus then intensifies the belief in the correctness of the position. This homogeneity is achieved mainly through polarization and through the communication and pooling of information.

Polarization

Polarization is one of the most powerful and widely re-searched phenomena in social psychology. Here is the basic finding: when people share a leaning in a certain direction and they discuss their views, they become more extreme in that direction. The direction, or "pole," could be a "guilty" or "not guilty" verdict; it could be advocacy for or against making a merger; it could be liking or disliking Americans. It could be an inclination to invade the Bay of Pigs.

Hundreds of studies have documented the fact that a group of people who basically agree on the direction of a decision will become more extreme and more confident after discussion. Groups of prejudiced people become more prejudiced. Groups of people prone to taking a given risk become more risky. Groups of people prone to caution become more cautious.

Polarization is one of those very predictable and well-documented consequences of discussing an issue with those who basically agree with us. And since we seek out people who agree with us, polarization occurs frequently. We may differ with them in degree or on the specifics, but that shared direction moves us toward the extreme.

Originally, this was found in studies on risk-taking. Groups frequently became more prone to risk-taking than their individual members, and this came to be called the "risky shift." Initially, researchers thought that this phenomenon was limited to risk, but they came to realize that it is far more general. It replicates over and over in very different situations. The history of how researchers came to understand the "risky shift" is interesting, in part because it shows the importance of testing the opposite of what a line of research had shown. In this case, they had to consider that the shift could be to caution rather than risk.

For some time, it was assumed that groups are generally more risky than the average of the individuals. The breakthrough in the research came from noticing that some groups did not become more prone to risk-taking. In fact, some groups became more cautious. Rather than consider this an aberration, some researchers carefully examined data that already existed. They then designed new studies that uncovered a more general phenomenon. In their examination of data, researchers found a pattern. On items where people favored risk, they became riskier after group discussion. Where they initially favored caution, group discussion led them to be more cautious. Either way, group discussion led them to become more extreme in their position—but more extreme in the direction they already favored.

To give you a flavor of the kinds of shifts that researchers discovered, one study had an item that asked participants whether a recent graduate should remain in his present but uninspiring job or take an exciting and better-paid job with a new firm that might fail. Participants tended toward risk on this item, and group discussion made them even more prone to risk. By contrast, another item described a man experiencing stomach problems at the airport who was deciding between seeing a doctor and abandoning his vacation plans or taking off on the charter flight with the risk of his condition getting worse. Here, participants tended toward caution. In groups, they were even more cautious. In many of these studies, a group might be only three people, and the discussion might last only a few minutes. Yet there was a shift to the extreme. And as we would later learn, this is not limited to issues involving risk-taking.

The recognition of the more general phenomenon came from studies conducted in France in the 1960s. The participants were French high school students who shared a leaning: they were pro–de Gaulle and anti-American. I remember this because I worked with the two authors in Paris the year that study was published—it was not a time when we Americans were embraced in France. That study found that discussion led to more extreme views on both parts of this leaning. These like-minded high schoolers became even more favorable to de Gaulle and even less favorable to Americans after discussion. With this study came the term "group polarization" to describe the more general phenomenon.

Other studies corroborated this tendency of like-minded groups to become more extreme and extended the analysis to other areas. For example, after discussion, groups of relatively racist individuals became *more* racist, and groups of relatively nonracist individuals became *less* racist.

The insights reached in these studies have also helped us to better understand the important research by Kurt Lewin that was part of the war effort during World War II.

> During the war, the populace was urged to change its eating habits because there was a shortage of protein sources such as beef, lamb, and pork. Citizens were encouraged to eat organ meats like tongue, liver, sweetbreads, and brains. Kurt Lewin, a social psychologist at the University of Iowa, was enlisted to help people make that change.

Lewin tried various methods to get families to at least try these protein-rich foods. He tried variations on the lecture method: teaching people about organ meats, giving them recipes, encouraging them to make the change for the war effort, and so on. He also tried another method: asking small groups to discuss the issue and decide whether they would try the organ meats. Almost everyone, regardless of condition, was inclined to try them. However, it was in the discussion condition that they actually did so. Compared to the lecture method, the discussion method won hands down in inducing the change in behavior. Participants in discussion groups tried the organ meats five times as often as those exposed to various lectures. <

Mothers, even those whose children were picky eaters, were not only more favorable toward preparing these new foods after they participated in a group discussion, but they did so. The take-home message is that a lecture can make you more inclined to do something, but it is group discussion where members lean in one direction that makes their views more extreme and where they act on those views. For people already leaning in one direction, then, discussing that view with those who have a similar leaning leads to more extreme attitudes, commitment to follow through on those attitudes, and actual behavior changes. In Lewin's study, the discussion group participants actually prepared and served the organ meats they were being urged to try.

Two prevailing theories have tried to explain why polarization occurs. One is called "persuasive arguments" theory. In its simplest terms, the arguments expressed in a group discussion favor the direction that most people have. If we all favor risk to a greater or lesser extent in a given situation, the comments in the group will argue for risk. Some of those arguments are ones we have already considered, but some are new. These will persuade us to go even further in our position. In the end, we will become more convinced, more extreme, and more confident.

The other theory is "social comparison" theory. Here the premise is that we want to be favorably viewed by members of our group, so we look to see what they value. We compare ourselves with the others. On average, we find that we are average. As a result, we move in the desired direction—we want to be just a little better than the others. If we all lean toward risk, for example, we each want to be a little more risk-taking than the others. One image that comes to mind is of leapfrogging to admiration.

The debates between the two theories prompted a good deal of research, and meta-analyses have generally confirmed that *both* theories have merit. The important message is that discussion among the like-minded leading to more extreme views in the shared direction is a powerful, highly replicable phenomenon.

Communication and Pooling Information

In the Bay of Pigs fiasco, polarization was likely operating. The like-minded individuals who leaned toward invasion became more convinced and more extreme in this view, and eventually they decided to implement that course of action. Another reason why polarization likely occurred is because of the information they shared—*or did not share*—while they were discussing the issue and making the decision.

A well-researched phenomenon in groups is that individuals share the information they have *in common*. Individuals are less likely to share information that is unique to them. For example, if only one person, or only a few, have certain information, it is less likely to be expressed and thus less likely to be part of the decision-making process.

One of the benefits of groups, we assume, is that they have more resources and a wider variety of information, experience, and knowledge on which to draw than any given individual does. But what if that valuable information is not shared? What if it is not expressed? An early study by Garold Stasser and William Titus demonstrated that groups do not effectively pool their information. The group thus has a biased sample of the information. What is expressed—what is put on the table during discussion—is information that members had *before* the discussion and information that favors their *current* position.

In Stasser and Titus's early study, a three-member group was to select the best hypothetical candidate for student body president. There were seven pieces of information that favored candidate A and four pieces that favored candidate B, so once the group pooled its information, it would have selected candidate A. However, the likelihood of that being the group's final selection depended on how that information was distributed among the individuals.

In one condition, each group member had all four pieces of information favoring candidate B, while the seven pieces of information favoring candidate A were distributed unevenly among them. Of these seven pieces favoring candidate A, everyone had one piece of information that was the same. The other six pieces of information favoring candidate A were distributed as pairs among the three group members. Thus, each had three pieces of information favoring candidate A, but not the same ones. Together, however, the group had all seven pieces of information favoring candidate A: if they pooled their information, they would select candidate A. They didn't do this. They did not share all the information and ended up making the wrong decision. Upon analysis, the reason for the poor decision is that they shared the information they had in common—which was primarily the four pieces of information favoring candidate B.

There might be several reasons for why the group members shared the information they held in common. They might have been defending their initial preference, which generally favored candidate B since each had four pieces of information favoring candidate B and only three pieces favoring candidate A. It could even be a statistical artifact. However, what is clear is that the information on the table favored what they held in common. They expressed the information that everyone had and they talked about that information. Here as elsewhere, unique information tended not to be discussed. One study showed this proportion to be as strong as three-to-one favoring information held in common.

This same pattern has been found in a study of three-person medical teams—a resident, an intern, and a third-year medical student. The three discussed the diagnosis of patients who had been interviewed in an emergency room setting. In the study, the patient interviews were edited so that some symptoms were seen by all three people while other symptoms were seen by only one of the three. Again, if they pooled the information, they would make the best decision.

An analysis of their discussions leading to a diagnosis showed that they mainly discussed the symptoms that all three knew. In fact, the *first* symptom that they discussed was almost always one they all knew about—one that was common to the group. The second symptom that they discussed had a 70 percent likelihood of being held in common. The point here is that the unique information—the symptom seen by only one of the three—was less likely to be discussed. Subsequent research shows that unique information is also less likely to be repeated during the course of a discussion.

You can see the implications for our medical world, especially when doctors are highly specialized. They have knowledge they hold in common with other doctors, but they also have unique knowledge. It is a special doctor— dare we say a "unique" doctor—who discusses his unique information with others.

One real-life situation shows how "common" knowledge can narrow the range of considerations and how unique knowledge can change the definition of the problem and thus the solution. When a patient developed a persistent pneumonia, she was sent to pulmonologists who did CT scans, prescribed antibiotics, and generally assured her that it would take time. After four months of continuing pneumonia, more scans, and several rounds of antibiotics, the pulmonologists talked to another one, and their common knowledge was that they were treating the pneumonia appropriately. One dared to opine that he was not worried because it was "going in the right direction." When asked why the pneumonia had not cleared after four months, he repeated: "I am not worried." Translation: *Don't question me.*

Fortunately, the patient's primary doctor had the unique information that she had a history of acid reflux as well as a large hiatal hernia—information that, by the way, was also available to the pulmonologists. Perhaps more importantly, the primary doctor took the question seriously: why was the pneumonia persisting after four months? He conveyed the unique information he had to various specialists. Linking what was common information with what was unique information, the primary doctor concluded that the pneumonia was caused by stomach acid entering the patient's lungs. This diagnosis led to a very different decision and a surgical solution to address the problem.

The tendency for groups to discuss primarily the information they have in common is one reason why groups can move too easily to consensus, and it was one reason why President Kennedy and his advisers made their disastrous decision to invade Cuba at the Bay of Pigs. By all accounts, information that would have cast doubt on the success of this course of action or that favored an alternative was not shared in that group.

The implications for dissenting views are apparent. Dissent, by definition, is a minority opinion, and the information that informs it is relatively unique. Being unique, this information is less likely to be expressed, less likely to be repeated, and less likely to enter the pool of information that will decide the outcome. It is worth remembering that Schlesinger did not share his unique information or opinion with others in the Bay of Pigs decision. He had many doubts and would later reproach himself for not speaking up.

From the point of view of good decision-making, this tendency to pool information that is held in common increases the likelihood that groups will miss an important piece of information. There are now many studies—collectively known as "hidden profile" studies—that have demonstrated this phenomenon. If some of the information is hidden—that is, not everyone knows it—it is less likely to be communicated or discussed. A meta-analysis of sixty-five studies that used "hidden profiles" concludes that such groups are eight times less likely to find the right solution compared to groups in which everyone knows all of the information.

The overarching insight of this work is that it is important to know how information is distributed. In the best situation, a piece of information that is known by one member of a group will become known by all members and the group will operate with the sum of its knowledge. After all, one of the presumed benefits of groups is that they have more diverse information, abilities, and perspectives. Once we realize that this benefit depends on how many people hold the same piece of information and who they are, we see once again the perils of majorities, and especially of consensus. Information held by the majority tends to be grossly overrepresented and repeated, making all the difference in the decision-making. One piece of unique information could change the whole picture and the final decision. And whether in the realm of justice or politics or hiring, this can have long-term consequences.

We have seen the power of consensus in different forms. Discussion among people who lean in the same direction leads to more extreme views. When information is held in common by people, they tend to share that information in the group, thus overemphasizing what they know in common. In more naturalistic decision-making settings, we repeatedly see that the desire to achieve consensus is a central problem—the Bay of Pigs decision being a prime example. In that case, the discussion was narrow and favored the perspective of the emerging consensus. What was missing, we will argue, was challenge, providing unique information and stimulating a consideration of alternatives.

LEARNING FROM FAILURE: JFK AND HIS CABINET

The ill-conceived plan of the Bay of Pigs showed all the elements of bad decision-making, but apparently the decision-makers learned from that experience. They had a chance to use what they learned in a crisis that erupted soon after. This was the Cuban Missile Crisis. Kennedy in particular showed an awareness of phenomena like polarization and information pooling and groupthink. Having learned the problems inherent in being a "directed leader," he removed himself from the deliberation. He and the team set about to give us an example of how groups can make *good* decisions.

▶ Fidel Castro of Cuba and Nikita Khrushchev of the Soviet Union had reached a deal to place Soviet nuclear missiles in Cuba in July 1962. US intelligence picked up evidence of a buildup and issued a warning. The warning went unheeded. Then came the pictures of missiles being built. President Kennedy summoned his advisers, many of whom were the same people who had been involved in the Bay of Pigs decision. With the same people as advisers, and the same adversary (Castro and Cuba), would there again be an invasion? It was considered. What would change in the decision-making this time around? As it turned out, plenty.

Several advisers, especially the Joint Chiefs of Staff, favored an invasion. Minimally, they advised air strikes. This time, instead of debating only the one plan, they followed a new decision-making approach that called for exploring options. For instance, someone suggested an alternative to invasion—a naval blockade to force the Soviets to remove the missiles.

Other changes in the decision-making process reportedly included JFK's instruction to his brother Bobby to lead a thorough deliberation of the two alternatives. The discussions were frank, and no one chaired the meeting. The advisers separated into two groups, and each wrote a position paper favoring one of the alternatives. Then they swapped papers. They dissented; they criticized the alternatives. Only then were the position papers presented to the president.

Martin Hansen, writing in the *Harvard Business Review*, refers to these changes in the process as lessons learned. Kennedy asked each member to be a "skeptical generalist." He had learned not to be a "directed leader." They sometimes met without him. He did not take part in all of the discussions, and he invited disagreement. The team fully embraced these principles as well. They had indeed learned some lessons from the Bay of Pigs fiasco.

This time around, more options and risks were considered, and arguments favoring each option were aired. In the end, Kennedy decided on a measured approach. He chose to quarantine Cuba, which was just short of a blockade. He wrote to Khrushchev and also informed the American public about his decisions and reasoning. He made clear that there would be retaliation against the Soviet Union if it launched a missile against any nation. Luckily, he had credibility that he would make good on his threats.

Khrushchev reacted to the quarantine by sending ships on October 24 and 25, 1962. Some turned back, while others were stopped. Kennedy reportedly was ready for war but preferred diplomacy for a little while longer. Then apparently Khrushchev showed real statesmanship by sending a message that recognized the possibility of the unthinkable—a thermonuclear war. Khrushchev suggested that both sides "relax the forces pulling on the ends of the rope," adding, "Let us take measures to untie that knot. We are ready for this."

By all accounts, the decision-making process during the Cuban Missile Crisis was very successful. War came close—very close—but it was averted. Though much credit should be given to Kennedy and Khrushchev, the decision-making process itself was very different than that of the Bay of Pigs decision. Kennedy understood the hazards of being a directed leader and instituted mechanisms for creating differences of opinion, considering the pros and cons, and engaging in serious open debate.

These mechanisms included separating groups into subgroups to invite the sharing of unique information. This likely reduced the "hidden" profiles of information. Other mechanisms included inviting disagreement, which helped the groups to avoid moving to the extremes. They were encouraged to argue against a position as well as argue for it. In all, Kennedy encouraged a culture of authentic dissent. He was applauded for his "combination of toughness and restraint, of will, nerve and wisdom." This was his finest hour, as it was for his team.

As I have written elsewhere, corporate cultures can aid good decision-making *and* innovation if they welcome authentic dissent. Kennedy's wisdom was in encouraging such a culture in the Cuban Missile Crisis, unlike in the Bay of Pigs decision, where he had opted for control and consensus.

These examples illustrate the power and value of a culture that values dissent. Such a culture increases the likelihood that the dissent will be expressed. Otherwise, it is more difficult for the dissenter to speak up. One can only speculate, but had Schlesinger actively spoken up about his reservations during the Bay of Pigs decision, the decision-making might have taken a different course, and the research shows us that we can assume it would have been a better course. We can only hope that future leaders will learn from the contrasts between two of the most important decisions the Kennedy team faced.

7 BETTER DECISIONS: DISSENT, DIVERSITY, AND DEVIL'S ADVOCATES

IN PRINCIPLE, GROUPS HAVE MORE RESOURCES THAN INDI-viduals—more information, experience, and perspective. Yet groups can operate as less than the sum of their parts when not all of those resources are brought to bear, not all information is expressed, and not all opinions are aired. The march to consensus favors the majority and what the individual group members know and believe in common. Thus, there can be a rush to judgment. Consensus leads the individuals to view information and opinions through the prism of "the many." What is often critically lost is any serious consideration of alternatives or reassessment of the preferred options. It should be no surprise, then, that the resulting decisions can be poor—and as we have seen, can sometimes be deadly.

Many researchers and consultants give advice on how to make "smart decisions." Most emphasize the need to "evaluate risks and benefits with equal vigor" and to "foster and address constructive criticism." Many recognize the value of candor and debate. They point to the problems, especially bias, and recognize the value of divergent thinking. However, after making the case for seeking advice, getting more or better training, and having good intentions, many people—researchers, practitioners, and laypeople alike—tell us that the real key to making good decisions is diversity or some kind of technique that plants dissent without needing a true dissenter.

THE FALSE PROMISE OF DIVERSITY

When most people speak of diversity, they often mean demographic diversity, especially legally mandated categories such as race, gender, and sexual orientation. Sometimes they add in age or tenure in an organization. Many people point to diversity as a way to counter the problems of demographic homogeneity, which bring to mind the teams of all-white, middle-aged men making decisions in the Oval Office during the Kennedy administration, or in executive boardrooms across the country. They argue that homogeneity impairs the quality of decision-making whereas diversity improves it. Research shows, however, that good team decision-making is far more complicated.

Same Facts, Different Conclusions

> In 1995, the trial of the century was held. O. J. Simpson, a famous celebrity and former running back for the Buffalo Bills, was accused of killing his ex-wife, Nicole Brown Simpson, and her friend Ron Goldman. In the criminal trial, O. J. was found "not guilty" of murder. A year later in a civil trial, he was found "guilty" of their wrongful deaths.

Nicole Brown Simpson and Ron Goldman were killed on June 13, 1994. It was a savage killing. There was a history of domestic abuse in the Simpsons' marriage. All three individuals—the two murder victims and Simpson himself—were very physically attractive. Racial tensions ran high throughout the trial and media coverage. O. J. was African American, and Nicole Brown Simpson and Ron Goldman were Caucasian. O. J. was charged with stabbing his ex-wife multiple times in the neck, one going so deep that it severed the jugular vein and both carotid arteries.

The crime occurred in Brentwood, part of the Santa Monica District of Los Angeles. Both of the Simpsons lived in the area, he in a sprawling mansion, she in a more modest house. Brentwood is an upscale, mostly white area. However, the trial was shifted to downtown Los Angeles, which is mostly black and much less wealthy.

This decision would change the jury pool. On October 3, 1995, after nine months of testimony, involving 45,000 pages of evidence, the jury deliberated less than four hours and returned a verdict of "not guilty." Some observers rejoiced, while others despaired. Many believed—and believe to this day—that Mr. Simpson was acquitted largely because the trial was held in downtown Los Angeles rather than Santa Monica. Racial bias was assumed to be at the heart of the verdict.

Most people believe that race played a strong part in the verdict, not necessarily because of outright prejudice but, rather, because the jurors interpreted the evidence through the lens of race. Looking at the same evidence, a jury in the wrongful death civil case came to a different verdict a year and a half later, administering a different kind of justice.

This civil trial was held in Santa Monica, the district where the crime was committed. After a three-month trial and seventeen hours of deliberation, the verdict was announced on April 4, 1997. The verdict was guilty. The jury awarded $8.5 million in compensatory damages to the Goldmans and $25 million in punitive damages to the Brown and Goldman families. Mr. Simpson vowed to never pay a penny of these awards, and succeeded in that. He moved to Florida where, by law, his $20,000 a month income from a pension fund was protected.

The two cases differed in a number of respects, such as the different burden of proof required in criminal versus

civil cases. Most analyses, however, focused on the importance of the venue. One favored African American jurors
and the other favored white jurors. In the criminal trial,
nine of the twelve jurors were black, one was Hispanic,
one was white, and one was half Native American and half
white. In the civil trial, the jury consisted of nine whites,
one Asian, one Hispanic, and one person of black and
Asian ancestry. A mostly black jury acquitted O. J. Simpson in the first trial, and a mostly white jury convicted him
in the second trial. Most people believe that race played
a large part in the different verdicts and that both whites
and blacks were biased in the direction that favored their
own race.

Which jury was right? Perhaps neither engaged in good
decision-making processes.

There is good reason to assume that people favor those
who are similar to themselves and who come from the
same category. In fact, sharing just a label, even an ar-
bitrary one, is enough for what researchers call in-group
favoritism—a preference for those with that element of
identity in common. We prefer people of our own group
to those in other groups, even if the group amounts to just
a label. For instance, when people were brought into a
laboratory and randomly grouped together as "the blues"
or "the greens," they were found to favor members of their
artificial group.

In the O. J. Simpson trials, there might have been a
straight outright vote based on race, but more likely there
were sympathies based on similarity of race. The jurors

likely interpreted the evidence through the lens of their shared experience—including beliefs such as whether police plant evidence or not.

Most assume that the large majority of one race or the other in the two trials directly translated into bias for or against O. J. Simpson. Thus, both juries were faulted for bias. Many who believe that the answer is diversity assume that, had the juries been more diverse—more racially balanced—the deliberation would have been less biased, there would have been counters to racial bias, and the decision-making process would have been better.

Whether a large majority of a given race biases the decision-making process is up for debate, but what is clear is that people perceive this to be the case and the perception of such bias has consequences. The city of Miami still remembers the 1980 case of four white police officers who were acquitted of killing a black insurance man, Arthur McDuffie. McDuffie ran a red light and was pursued by several policemen. Newspapers reported, "As many as a dozen officers beat him into a coma. He died in the hospital." There had already been outrage, but when the officers were acquitted by an all-white jury, the community erupted. By some accounts, the ensuing three days of riots led to 18 deaths, 350 injuries, and over $100 million in damages.

More recently, on August 9, 2014, there were days of uprisings in Ferguson, Missouri, when a young black man, Michael Brown, was shot and killed by a white police officer, Darren Wilson. There was inconsistency in the initial reports, but some witnesses said that Brown was unarmed and had his hands up while surrendering to police. There were not only protests but rioting and vandalism that lasted for weeks. A grand jury was quickly convened, and it delivered its verdict on November 24, 2014. Deciding that the matter "lacks prosecutive merit and should be closed," the grand jury's decision was to not indict Darren Wilson. Further protests and unrest ensued.

The point here is not whether these decisions were right or wrong or whether they were racially biased, but that there was a perception of racial bias and that such perceptions have significant consequences. This perception of bias is likely to arise when the category and the vote coincide—for example, when an all-white jury acquits a white defendant of killing a black man, as in Miami, or a largely black jury acquits O. J. Simpson while a largely white jury convicts him. What would be different if we made sure there was diversity in our groups or juries?

Diversity might improve the *perception* that the correct decision was reached, but does it actually improve the decision-making process? Does it correct biases? Those who argue for diversity often see it as a mechanism for providing different perspectives and assume that would be a corrective to bias. As to the first point, demographic diversity does not ensure diversity of perspective. The fact that a group includes men and women, a mix of races and ethnicities, people of different educational and socio-economic levels, and so forth, doesn't ensure heterogeneity of opinion or perspective.

To make this point, I often show my classes photographs of the cabinets of George W. Bush and Barack Obama. Both cabinets show a mix of demographics: men and women, a range of ethnicities and races, and even different heights, weights, and, to some extent, ages. As an aside, the one thing I noticed is that they don't differ much in the type and color of their attire; for men, the blue suit is still de rigueur, albeit with a little diversity in the color of the tie. The one thing I can almost guarantee is that the cabinet members in either administration do not differ much in their political leanings or perspectives on policy. They were chosen for their loyalty to the president and their alignment with his vision.

The homogeneity of a demographic category, on the other hand, does not necessarily mean homogeneity of perspective. Not all whites would have convicted O. J., nor would all African Americans have acquitted him. Not all African Americans would have indicted Darren Wilson. Most people believe, however, that race is correlated with a leaning or direction. It is not far-fetched to assume that blacks will be more likely than whites to believe that the police fabricate evidence (such as the bloody glove) or to have "reasonable doubt" about the guilt of a black man (O. J.). Many would argue that diversity—a better balance of race and socioeconomic status among the jurors—would have increased debate and improved the decision-making processes in both juries. It most surely would have increased the perception of a fair verdict, but the evidence does not support the notion that diversity of category actually leads to better-quality decision-making.

Given the importance of this distinction between category diversity and opinion diversity, it is not surprising that the research shows mixed results for the link between demographic diversity and the quality of team performance or decision-making. Many teams with diverse categories do not have diverse perspectives. Some have diverse perspectives, but team members do not speak up. The studies demonstrate that having a diverse mix of demographic categories may or may not improve group decision-making. In some cases, diversity can have other effects, some of which are considered negative.

Studies show that diversity of demographics can *lower* morale and bonding, which many organizations try to avoid. It can also reduce satisfaction and even retention. Since there is repeated evidence that similarity is a powerful predictor of liking, high morale, and friendships, demographic diversity poses challenges. It can create "we/they" divides. It can also make communication more difficult— or at least more complex.

You might think that it is more beneficial to have diversity of some categories rather than others. Is gender diversity of more value than age diversity for team performance? Again, the numerous studies and even meta-analyses of the research paint a disappointing picture. The conclusion is that "neither diversity on readily observable attributes nor diversity on underlying job-related attributes could be reliably linked to group performance." Note the adverb "reliably." It isn't that some studies don't show a positive relationship between certain categories of diversity and some element of performance or good decision-making. Some do, but others show a negative relationship or no relationship. In a specific case, we can find strong effects, but as a general pattern, the value of demographic diversity for the quality of decision-making or performance is mixed. To some extent, then, demographic diversity is a "false promise" if we expect it to have consistent beneficial effects on the quality of decisions or on general morale.

I think the key to the benefits of diversity for decision-making lies in whether it actually brings different perspectives into the process. Katherine Williams and Charles O'Reilly, professors at Columbia and Stanford Business Schools, respectively, asked this fundamental question, namely, "whether increased diversity actually adds valuable problem-solving perspectives and information." These benefits don't come automatically just from having a mix of categories. Neither of the diverse cabinets of George W. Bush and Barack Obama was a "team of rivals." The two presidents did not look for people who had views that differed from their own. In fact, they searched for the opposite—a mix of people from the right demographics, but with the same basic ideology.

The Search for Diversity of Perspective

Some companies actively seek diversity of experience or opinion. Several executives whom I interviewed fervently believe in diversity—but they look beyond demographic diversity. What they seek is diversity of background or perspective. Perhaps more importantly, they welcome the expression of different views. Here are several illustrations:

> ▶ Carrie Schwab-Pomerantz, head of the Charles Schwab Foundation, is passionate about financial literacy for women and low-income individuals. She spoke eloquently to me about the importance of having team members with different backgrounds, but importantly, having differing skills and ideas. "You're not looking for people who are just like you. You're looking for people who are better than you in certain areas, who can offer new insight and fill in the gaps." Understandably, one of her favorite books is *Team of Rivals: The Political Genius of Abraham Lincoln* by Doris Kearns Goodwin. Unafraid of having his own power usurped, Abraham Lincoln sought out the best people for his cabinet, including his chief rivals.
>
> Some companies, such as the wonderfully creative IDEO, use diversity to their advantage. IDEO searches for diversity of skill and knowledge rather than readily observable demographics. In a tour of the San Francisco office, Whitney Mortimer, partner and chief marketing officer, relayed the principles and strategy at IDEO. The company's strategy is human-centered, and the service is design. They don't make products. They help us to use them. To do this well, IDEO needs diversity, but the most useful kind is diversity of skill, knowledge, and background.

Several companies use techniques to tap diverse backgrounds or experiences by "walking in the shoes" of the consumer. IDEO might, for example, have an employee spend time in a hospital bed looking at the ceiling to see it from the perspective of the patient. Intuit uses a similar mechanism. Scott Cook, founder of Intuit, has found considerable value in the technique of walking in the shoes of the user of his financial software. So has his senior vice president of marketing, Nora Denzel. They both relayed to me that following people around as they use a product or just watching how they use it can provide insights. Intuit has even used this technique on train platforms near company headquarters. Walking in the consumer's shoes can point out problems as people try to use a product or a service. It can also be a source of new ideas.

Catherine Lelong, who worked at Wolff Olins, a world leader in branding and identity, told me about that company's great emphasis on diversity of background. Except for some who have specific technical expertise, teams are intentionally made up of members from very different backgrounds. She gave me one example of how homogeneity can create silos of thought. If team members are all engineers, they might think that a variant on a new product should be called C13, since they came up with it on their thirteenth try. Non-engineers know that this name is unlikely to inspire anyone to buy the product.   ◁

Her point is well taken. Apple products, for example, have numbers such as OS X 10.9, OS X 10.10, and OS X 10.12, but they go by the names of Mavericks, Yosemite, and El Capitan. Who doesn't want to be a Maverick or climb El Capitan in Yosemite—even if we are barely able to climb stairs?

Some executives recognize that diversity of background and perspective is important but that opinion differences, when they exist, need to be communicated. Diversity might provide a range of views, but to have value, those views need to be expressed—perhaps even welcomed in a debate between views. For this to happen, however, there must be a leader who actually welcomes differences in viewpoint.

▶ This may be one reason for the effectiveness of executives such as Jenny Johnson, President and Chief Operating Officer of Franklin Resources. She may be one of the most open people I know when it comes to seeking out differing views. When she observes the reticence of a team member, she solicits his or her views. For Jenny, seeing all sides is the route to "true North." Her reaction to challenge is not defensive. Rather, it is curious, for she remains focused on goals and "getting it right." That is the advice of her grandfather and father, who founded and led Franklin Resources, the parent company of Franklin Templeton. That advice, as she told me, was to "put the client first. Everything else takes care of itself." With a long history of philanthropy, that family guidance may also be one reason why she invites views that are not only applicable to finance but include issues of ethics and compassion. ◁

The important point of these examples is that not only do they show an appreciation for the benefits of different backgrounds but they recognize the importance of different perspectives being expressed. By word and deed, these leaders seek and welcome the expression of differing points of view.

In summary, as the research shows, diversity of demographics bears an unreliable relationship to team decision-making and performance. Diversity of perspective or opinion bears more promise, provided the differences are expressed. We would argue that the benefits are especially likely if the differences involve a minority viewpoint, one that challenges the prevailing consensus.

If someone challenges the prevailing position or mode of thinking, the evidence supports the notion that other people will be more likely to act independently—to "know what they know" and to speak up. As we saw in Chapter 5, those other people will also be stimulated to think divergently—the exact kind of thinking that leads to good decision-making.

The bottom line is that we might want a mix of people on our teams. We might want people who vary in age, race, gender, ethnicity, and sexual orientation—and maybe educational background, height and weight, and personality for that matter. There are many good reasons for this, but there is little evidence that it will improve performance or decision-making by itself. The value is found in the persistent expression of a differing view, which stimulates thought about the decision at hand. Diversity in its many forms may provide the potential for improving decisions, but the real engine for good decision-making is dissent.

THE BEST ANTIDOTE: DISSENT

Twelve Angry Men without Henry Fonda would have been *Eleven Angry Men* who rushed to the judgment that the defendant was guilty—and, most surely, that verdict would have taken them minutes, not hours, to reach. Any lone dissenter would most probably have capitulated, at least eventually. As to the quality of the deliberation, we probably would have seen convergent thinking and a groupthink kind of process. Instead, that film showed the power of dissent, of that one persistent minority voice. In Chapter 3, we saw the ways in which Fonda, as the dissenter, persuaded others to his position. However, as demonstrated in Chapter 5, dissent is useful not just in persuasion but in stimulating divergent thinking, the kind of thinking which is necessary for good decision-making. Without dissent, that jury's discussion would most likely have reflected convergent thinking and a rush to judgment—the kind of thinking that leads to bad decisions, as reported in Chapter 6.

The value of dissent for the quality of group decisions has also been studied in more naturalistic settings. For example, Linn Van Dyne of Michigan State and Richard Saavedra of Carnegie Mellon conducted a field study in which groups of four or five met over a ten-week period. Some groups included a person who had been trained to be a persistent minority voice. The other groups had no such trained dissenter. Those groups that experienced dissent reported more divergent thinking. They "identi- fied a large number of alternatives" or "identified many advantages and disadvantages to each alternative." They also produced reports that were consistently rated as more original and of better quality by outside experts.

One of the most ambitious naturalistic studies observed the value of dissent for strategic decision-making in US hospitals. With all the challenges posed by a large field study, the researchers surveyed the entire population of hospitals in three states. They found evidence that when members "openly expressed a difference of opinion," the quality of the decision was better. Such decisions were seen as more financially responsible and as contributing to the hospital's overall effectiveness.

The results of studies of top management teams by Kathleen Eisenhardt and her colleagues are consistent with these studies. They concluded that it is often valuable to "have a good fight" in decision-making teams. Among the tactics of the best teams are that "they work with more, rather than less, information. They develop multiple alternatives to enrich debate. They resolve issues without forcing them to consensus."

Even the US Supreme Court provides evidence for the value of dissent. Dissent has been found to increase what is called the integrative complexity of the Court's decisions. This concept is akin to divergent thinking. Integrative complexity is the ability to see both sides of an issue and their trade-offs. One study of Supreme Court decisions analyzed its written opinions for integrative complexity and found that they showed more of it when there was a dissenting opinion. When the Court's opinion was written on behalf of a unanimous group, it showed significantly low integrative complexity. When the opinion of the Court was written on behalf of a majority who confronted a dissenting opinion, the integrative complexity was high. It was in the latter case that the justices showed an awareness of alternatives and were more likely to consider both sides—at least in their written arguments.

Given the evidence, both experimentally and in natural settings, that dissent stimulates the kind of thinking that makes for good decision-making, we must ask why so many people do not embrace it and even resist it. The reason, I suspect, is that people want to avoid conflict. They believe, or have been persuaded, that the route to good team functioning lies in liking and cohesion—precisely the factors that promote a rush to judgment. We are repeatedly advised "to go along and to get along" if we are to "win friends and influence people." Dissent involves conflict. It makes people uncomfortable and invokes their anger and dislike of the dissenter. On top of this, people do not credit the dissenter with stimulating divergent thinking. They certainly do not recognize the impact of dissent on their own thinking.

For many people, perhaps most people, the value of dissent lies almost totally in the outside possibility that it might be correct. Sometimes the dissenting view *is* correct, and as we have seen, sometimes the majority will be persuaded. Jeffrey Sonnenfeld, the well-known professor at Yale, relates the story of a dissenter at Medtronic who convinced the company's board and Bill George, its former CEO, to reverse themselves and "not get out of the angioplasty business—and, indeed to intensify those services . . . [which] paid off handsomely." For many people, this possibility—that the dissenting view might be right—is the reason they listen to the dissenter, but only for a while.

What goes unrecognized is that dissent stimulates divergent thinking in us as members of the majority even when it's wrong. We are stimulated to think divergently regardless of the merit of the dissenting position.

Many people recognize the importance of divergent thinking and yet still resist the solution of dissent as the vehicle for it. They want a mechanism that will clone the stimulating effects of dissent, but without the conflict or dislike between team members that dissent engenders. High on their list of techniques for achieving divergent thinking is playing devil's advocate, a form of "pretend dissent." This wishful thinking may be one reason why it has been heavily utilized, but without sufficient scrutiny.

Recent books like Tom Kelley's *The Ten Faces of Innovation* also try to avoid conflict and even take it a step further. They go so far as to suggest that even the devil's advocate technique is too negative and "idea stifling." They thus join the chorus advocating harmony and role-playing as routes to creativity and good decision-making. Instead, we suggest that the need is for challenge and debate—the curious ways of thinking that are stimulated by authentic dissent. It is worthwhile to explore these contrasting views and, in particular, to investigate the widely utilized technique of devil's advocate.

COMPOUNDING A FALSE PROMISE: THE DOWNSIDES OF PLAYING DEVIL'S ADVOCATE

The origins of the devil's advocate technique lie in the practice of the Roman Catholic Church when considering a candidate for sainthood. Understandably, the Vatican doesn't want to make a mistake. They don't want to learn later that the candidate for sainthood behaved in ways that were not saintly. Thus, in 1587, they instituted a practice of exploring everything negative about the candidate. God's advocate might argue for the canonization, but the devil's advocate argued against it. He might argue that all the miracles attributed to the candidate, for example, were fraudulent.

The devil's advocate is a mechanism aimed at making sure that the cons, the reasons for not canonizing a person, are considered and not just the pros. Intuitively, the technique would seem to counterbalance a bias in favor of the candidate held by most of the decision-makers, including the Pope. It is worth remembering, however, that the devil's advocate is but one mechanism used in the process of canonization, which can take decades, if not centuries, to complete.

In modern uses of the technique, the premise is still that it will challenge consensus. Devil's advocate was the antidote favored by Irving Janis in discussing ways to counter groupthink. The greater hope is that this technique will stimulate some form of divergent thinking, the kind that, as we have seen, occurs with dissent and is directly linked to good decision-making. Minimally, the hope is that devil's advocate, like dissent, will encourage teams to "evaluate risks and benefits with equal vigor." It doesn't.

The devil's advocate has been the darling of researchers trying to find an antidote to groupthink symptoms, as Janis had in mind in his original formulation. In the more than forty years since, the technique has been regularly cited as one of the ways to help groups make good decisions. Executive education programs at major business schools regularly teach it as a valuable technique. It is assumed to be an effective mechanism, but this is yet another example of assumptions going unexamined.

Available research on the devil's advocate technique provides support for its value—*compared to groups where there is no challenge.* That is, compared to groups with no counterpositions, it can provide benefit. So, too, can its sister technique, dialectical inquiry, in which a person doesn't just argue all the negatives of a proposed position but also offers a counterposition. By and large, the two techniques do not reliably differ in their effectiveness, but are better than no challenge at all.

Any effectiveness of a devil's advocate most likely lies in the value of considering the negatives of a position, namely those offered by the devil's advocate. In that sense, it is akin to the technique of "considering the opposite," which has shown some promise in lowering bias in judgments.

While the devil's advocate technique appears to have some value, that value hasn't generally been scrutinized or compared to the effects of authentic dissent. Researchers and authors seem to assume that a "nice" version of dissent— playing devil's advocate or even role-playing as described in *The Ten Faces of Innovation*—is more likely to invite consideration of the dissenter's position. They seem not to recognize the power of dissent to stimulate a consideration of the cons as well as the pros of a position, as we noted in Chapter 5. The differences between these techniques and authentic dissent, however, run deeper than this.

We first conducted a study comparing the devil's advocate technique to authentic dissent in 1998. That first study was motivated by my belief that we don't seriously reexamine our positions because of good intentions or intellectual machinations. I had been skeptical about the devil's advocate for years. It seemed to me to be a contrivance. Anyone can undertake an intellectual game, but this is not the same as really thinking through all the pros and cons of something we believe.

I had also studied the power of authentic dissent for years and saw its ability to stimulate a broader search for information, a consideration of more alternatives, the usage of multiple strategies, and more original thinking. Those studies, which involved people questioning themselves and their opinions as they tried to find the truth, showed the importance of challenge and courage. Before we undertook our studies of the devil's advocate, I had never believed that you can role-play dissent and get those kinds of reactions.

Having expressed doubt for years, I would often question the efficacy of the devil's advocate whenever I taught groupthink and the suggested antidotes. I would find myself telling the class what I believed. Everyone assumed that these techniques worked, or that they were at least better than no dissent. To me, they were no more than intellectual exercises and not that different from the "polite and academic" conversation that I'd studied twenty-five years earlier with juries that operated under a majority rule. There I had found that once there were enough votes and the verdict was a foregone conclusion, the discussion became polite and academic. It no longer featured the robust conflict that the dissenting Supreme Court justices desired. Was playing devil's advocate just another version of engaging in polite and academic conversation? Or could it actually replicate the stimulating effects found with dissent—but with the added benefit of harmony? Having expressed doubts for years, I undertook the first study when three graduate students at Berkeley expressed their interest in testing these propositions.

This study was quite simple. We studied groups consisting of four individuals. In one set of groups, there was no dissent. In a second set, there was authentic dissent. In a third set, there was devil's advocate "dissent." To hold the arguments constant, and all communication as well, we had the four individuals in each group seated at a table and separated by partitions. They communicated via computer. They were aware of each other but could not communicate directly, either verbally or nonverbally. All the communication was done via the computers, which we could control.

The individuals "deliberated" a personal injury case and were to agree on compensation for "pain and suffering," since the medical costs and lost wages had already been covered in the case. They could choose any one of eight options in $75,000 increments. The lowest was $1 to $75,000, then $75,001 to $150,000; the eighth option was "over $525,000." They typed in their own position. From pretesting this case, we knew that they all would pick a low compensation. They did. All took the first or second position, and everyone's position was below $150,000.

Each person saw the arguments of each of the others, but in fact all of these arguments were preprogrammed. Each learned on the first ballot that two others agreed with her, favoring a position of low compensation. What

differed was whether a third individual, person B, agreed
with her as well (the no dissent condition) or took a different position of high compensation (being then a dissenter).
That "dissent," however, was either "authentic"—that is, it
was the true opinion of person B—or the result of person
B being asked by the experimenter to play devil's advocate. The arguments were identical.

After deliberation, each participant listed her thoughts
about the case. This technique has been found to be
very useful in tracking the thinking of individuals. These
thoughts were coded for quantity and also for whether they
were "internal" (coming from the individual) or "external"
(paraphrases of others' comments or the case material).
They were also coded for the direction of the thinking. Did
the thinking favor the person's own position, or did it consider both sides of the issue?

In general, those individuals who faced authentic dissent had the most internal thoughts. They themselves
were generating the thoughts, rather than paraphrasing
others or the case information. They were thinking. More
important was the direction of their thoughts. Those facing authentic dissent showed a balance in considering both
sides of the issue. Those facing a devil's advocate did not.
They had more thoughts *supporting their own position* than
did those facing authentic dissent. Rather than stimulating
thought on both sides of the issue, the devil's advocate
actually stimulated more thoughts in the participants that
defended their original position. It was not the kind of

thinking that proponents of the devil's advocate technique would have hypothesized or desired.

The whole point of the devil's advocate is to get people to consider the downsides as well as the upsides of their preferred position. It appears to do the reverse. Those facing a devil's advocate seem to be convincing themselves that they were right all along. By contrast, authentic dissent fostered the balance between the pros and cons of a position.

When I first presented this study at the "Knowledge and the Firm" conference at Berkeley, Dorothy Leonard, a Harvard Business School professor, confessed that she had been arguing for the devil's advocate technique in her executive education courses for years. She took our findings to heart and promptly incorporated them into her teaching and books. Our findings had shown that there is a reason to be cautious about the devil's advocate technique, including unintended negative consequences. Fortunately, executive education in business schools now includes a healthier skepticism about these role-playing forms of challenge.

A second study took this a step further. We wanted to compare authentic dissent to the devil's advocate in their impact, not just on thinking but on the solutions they generated. We also wanted to test some questions related to variants on the devil's advocate. For example, was it important for the advocate's true position to be known? Did it matter whether the advocate's true position coincided with what she was arguing as a devil's advocate? We were especially interested in seeing whether the technique could have the same impact as authentic dissent when there was the closest possible match, namely when the devil's advocate was known to believe the position she was asked to argue. Most would have predicted that this congruence would clone the effects of dissent. It didn't.

In this study, we compared authentic dissent to three versions of the devil's advocate. In one, the devil's advocate's own position was unknown. In a second, it was known to be the opposite of what the devil's advocate was asked to role-play by the experimenter. In other words, she held similar beliefs as the majority but role-played the opposite. In a third, her position was known to be the same as what she was asked to role-play. She actually believed what she was now arguing as a devil's advocate.

The comparison of most interest was between this third condition—a devil's advocate arguing a position she actually believed—and the authentic dissent condition, in which she argued the same position—the same way—but had not been asked to be a devil's advocate. In both of those conditions, she was arguing something she had believed from the beginning—and everyone knew it. The arguments were exactly the same, since they were scripted. The only difference was whether or not she had been asked to be a devil's advocate.

The four individuals in each group deliberated a management issue for eight rounds. Everyone could see the comments on their computer screen. In the "authentic dissent" condition and in each of the three devil's advocate conditions, the dissenter was an accomplice of the experimenter and was typing in comments from a prewritten script. The comments were identical for all conditions. After the deliberation, the participants were asked to give as many solutions as possible that would solve the particular management problem. We coded the responses for the number of solutions they provided and the quality of those solutions.

The results were surprising in a couple of ways. Most everyone expected substantial differences between the devil's advocate conditions. Most expected it would matter whether the devil's advocate position was known or unknown and whether she believed the position she was arguing or believed the reverse. The results showed that it made no difference on any measure. None of the versions of the devil's advocate caused significant differences in the quantity or quality of the solutions that the participants generated. Authentic dissent was the one condition—and the only one—where individuals came up with more solutions. They also came up with more creative solutions, which we measured by a combination of quality and quantity. It was authentic dissent that won hands down, even when compared to the condition where the devil's advocate argued what she believed—and the others knew that. Remember: this involved believing the same position and giving the same arguments in support of that position. Though seemingly identical to the authentic dissent condition, asking the person to play the devil's advocate eliminated the benefits for creative problem-solving.

Upon reflection, we have identified some of the problems inherent in the devil's advocate technique. Role-playing does not show the courage and conviction of authentic dissent. When a person is role-playing, you don't really know the relationship between what he is saying and what he believes. Even when his words are consistent with his beliefs, you know that he is *acting*. And since you are aware that he is playing a role, you are likely to think and interact with him differently. After all, you can't persuade someone who is role-playing to change his position.

Regardless of the reasons, the devil's advocate, unlike authentic dissent, does not stimulate the kinds of thinking that lead to good decision-making or creative problem-solving. We again see the importance of authentic expression of a dissenting view. Its power and ability to stimulate divergent thinking and creativity do not appear to be reproducible through role-playing or "pretend" forms of dissent.

Some researchers are convinced by this conclusion, but others have sought to improve the devil's advocate technique by amplifying the debate aspect of it. Among the solutions offered by Cass Sunstein and Reid Hastie, for example, is a pumped-up version of devil's advocate, called "red teaming," in which teams compete and try to defeat one another. Many other variants on role-playing also try to clone the properties of dissent, but what they often lack, almost by definition, is authenticity.

It is when you face a dissenter who believes his position, has the courage to say so, and does so persistently that you confront the possibility that you may be wrong.

You at least start to investigate the complexity of the information and the issue. You start to seek information and to consider alternatives, much as you do when first forming an opinion. You look at all sides. You consider the cons as well as the pros. You consider multiple possibilities. You aren't chitchatting, making friends, or engaging in an intellectual exercise—you are thinking. Pretend dissent does not stimulate such thinking. In fact, the early study reviewed here showed that "pretend" dissent can lead to thinking that bolsters the initial position rather than stimulating thought that considers the cons of a position.

The one thing you learn as a social psychologist is that we all have biased and inflated beliefs about our own rationality and independence. We think that we assess information fairly and rationally. We generally think that we are relatively unbiased and that knowledge coupled with good intentions will lead to truth. What you further learn is that you, like everyone else, select information and consider alternatives in a limited fashion. What you learn is how imperfect you are and how often you fail. Training and education may be helpful, but they, too, are inadequate. Learning and good intentions won't save us from biased thinking and poor judgments. A better route is to have our beliefs and ways of thinking directly challenged by someone who authentically believes differently than we.

Some firms have taken this approach to heart by creating processes that build dissent into their stages of decision-making. Finchwood Capital, a fairly new hedge fund, is one such organization. I had the occasion to interview its founder, Ankur Luthra, along with his senior analyst, Brendan Nemeth. They have thought carefully about their decision-making processes.

> Many firms think in terms of smart individuals who come up with good ideas. Luthra and Nemeth instead recognize the importance of process and are especially attuned to the importance of combating bias. Their process is thoughtful and replicable. Luthra, with his engineering background, expects the process to be data-driven.

Take their idea-generation process. Finchwood Capital has a theme day when they discuss an entire sector—for example, Internet security—and consider which companies will be the likely winners and losers in that sector. After researching that investment space as well as specific stocks, a lead proponent creates a one-off paper of the investments considered promising.

The interesting part of their process from the perspective of this book is that the proponent formally addresses the downsides of his position. He outlines the risks in a section known as the "Pre Mortem." This is a section on how the firm could lose money on the investment. The Pre Mortem is just the first step, however, in considering the downsides. Next steps include defending the proposal with colleagues who have read the paper. Only then is a decision made on whether to dig more deeply into the company under consideration.

This deeper diligence stage involves two key papers: an investment memo and a contra memo. The contra memo is a much deeper examination of the risks associated with the investment. It is written from the perspective of someone who opposes the investment. For example, if Finchwood wants to buy stock XYZ (a long position), this memo argues for "shorting" that stock. This is more than an intellectual exercise. It is a mechanism that gets closer to authentic dissent. In this case, the proponent is also the dissenter. He is expected to write a thoughtful and persuasive paper arguing the contra position. What is expected is not just a couple of paragraphs after a half-hour of thought, or five bullet points on how the firm could lose money on the investment, but an eight- to nine-page position paper that others read and to which they will respond. Argumentation and debate are highly encouraged.

The contra paper and ensuing discussion appear to have been very instrumental in Finchwood's success. However, their process is of special interest here because they give some evidence that confrontation with dissent leads to divergent thinking. In one example recounted by Luthra and Nemeth, they were considering an investment in a software company. Let's call it ABC. The company had shown rapid revenue growth with a very efficient sales and marketing model. Luthra and Nemeth were both very positive toward this investment, but per their process, they wrote a contra memo. There they laid out the arguments for the opposite of their own position to invest in the company. Their reasoning included the thesis that the competition, which in past years had fallen flat, would heat up in the near future, and that Microsoft in particular would be in a position to dominate the space with its latest release.

Luthra and Nemeth were comfortable with buying ABC because they had done due diligence. They had downloaded and tried out the competitor products, including Microsoft's, and were convinced that ABC's product was superior. That was a good enough reason to buy it. However, the contra memo stimulated their thinking about the future and other possibilities. Having found a signpost, they decided to check the competition regularly and be especially vigilant should Microsoft announce a new offering. They now had a measured position, one subject to change should certain events arise.

It turns out that Microsoft did later launch an updated version of its competing product—and Finchwood was attentive, thanks to the thinking stimulated by the contra memo. They downloaded the new Microsoft product and tested it rigorously, something they learned that other investors rarely did. They found it to be much improved, discussed it thoroughly, and decided that now the risks outweighed the benefits. They sold ABC, avoiding significant losses. Investors began to see that the competition had caught up. However, Finchwood had an advantage because it had the signposts generated by thinking that had been stimulated by writing and discussing a dissenting opinion. This process is not exactly the same as authentic dissent, but it is close.

Even the Roman Catholic Church, in a historical turn-around, has started to embrace dissent, abandoning its reliance on the devil's advocate method. When the route to sainthood was streamlined in 1983, the Church eliminated the traditional position of the devil's advocate. Some worried that doing so would leave little room for dissenting opinions. However, in an interesting variation, the Church invited authentic dissent from the fiercest critic of the next person being considered for sainthood— Mother Teresa, the Roman Catholic nun with the Missionaries of Charity in Calcutta. An international icon, she had been widely applauded for helping the poorest of the poor in India and those dying of diseases such as AIDS and leprosy.

That fierce critic was none other than Christopher Hitchens—essayist, author, and religious, literary, and social critic. Known for his confrontational style, Hitchens had criticized Mother Teresa and had even called her a fraud. He was asked to argue against her, and he did so with great flourish. One of his criticisms was that she wanted to convert people to her Roman Catholic beliefs, which Hitchens considered less than saintly.

Much to its credit, the Church had abandoned the devil's advocate technique and instead invited input from a true dissenter, one who authentically differed. They even listened to him. In the end, they decided that "his argument was irrelevant." However, I suspect that his critique stimulated a better scrutiny of the evidence and better decision-making.

8 CONCLUSIONS

THE UNDERLYING MESSAGE OF THIS BOOK IS TWOFOLD. Consensus, while comforting and harmonious as well as efficient, often leads us to make bad decisions. Dissent, while often annoying, is precisely the challenge that we need to reassess our own views and make better choices. It helps us consider alternatives and generate creative solutions. Dissent is a liberator.

So why do we punish dissent? Most of us believe that we are open to differing views. Some of us believe that we like challenges to our ideas. In practice, however, most of us dislike a person who believes the opposite of a position we hold, and we creatively look for reasons for his "error." We tend to think of him in negative terms. He is a trouble-maker who is wasting time and blocking our goals. We are quite willing to punish him, most often through ridicule or rejection.

We are continually advised "to go along and to get along." It is powerful advice for most of us who prefer to be "in" rather than "out." We like being accepted and valued—and we know that if we stand up against the majority, we will be "on the outs." We thus remain silent. Sometimes we even nod in agreement, not knowing why we are nodding—because we choose not to ask ourselves what we really be-lieve. There is a price for this as well.

This book applauds dissent, not for the truth it may hold, but for its impact on the way we think. Confronted by dissent, we are less likely to rush to judgment, whether as individuals or in groups. We are more likely to consider the pros *and* the cons of a position. Dissent, by and large, helps us make better decisions and come up with more creative solutions.

There are downsides to dissent, to be sure. Dissent in-creases conflict and sometimes lowers morale. It takes lon-ger to discuss options and analyze them. However, there is a trade-off, and that trade-off is a positive one. As long as the dissent is authentic, it becomes a mechanism for reexamining our positions and looking more extensively for information. What has always appealed to me is the finding that these beneficial outcomes occur *even if the dis-*

sent is wrong. Even then, dissent makes us more open to learning, to growing, and to changing.

WHAT THIS BOOK IS *NOT* ABOUT

Many people, in thinking about dissent and dissenters, have an image of an angry person, with arms flailing. Try Googling images for "dissenters." Some are photos of long-haired hippies or the Captain America bike from an earlier era. You will see images of people with stern, angry faces and fists raised. Some are marching to the guillotine or being beaten to a pulp. Cartoons often show the dissenter as someone both vulnerable and deserving of ridicule. Many of these images have business settings. For example, one shows a boss at the head of the table in an oversized chair. Three others line the sides of the table. The boss says, "I realize you were just saying what everyone was thinking . . . and if you do it again you're fired." Another shows an individual in a stockade and a coworker saying, "Things would go a lot better for you if you would simply agree with the boss's ideas." In still another, the boss (much in the vein of Mao Zedong's invitation to "let a hundred flowers blossom") says, "I encourage dissent. That way I can get rid of anyone who doesn't agree with me."

Most images portray the dissenter as an "outsider" to society and illustrate the repercussions of that position. A few portray dissent in positive terms—as patriotic and even courageous. One image shows hundreds of men with arms outstretched while one man has his arms folded, with the caption: "A lone dissenter risks his life by refusing to give Hitler the Nazi salute during The Third Reich's rule." The first thought that comes to mind is: what is going to happen to that one man?

It Is *Not* About Anger

Despite the impression given by these images of dissenters, the research covered in this book is not about anger. It is about the willingness of an individual, or a few, to express an opinion that challenges the majority view. Dissenters may provoke anger, but they are not expressing anger. They are expressing an opinion or perspective. To be effective, they need to be consistent and persistent, and it is undoubtedly better to do so with conviction, not anger. In *Twelve Angry Men*, Henry Fonda never yells or flails his arms. He calmly and consistently defends his position over time.

It Is *Not* About Diversity of Background

There are many reasons for having diversity of demographics on our teams, but the notion that this will improve decision-making is not one of them. The value lies in whether those team members bring and express different perspectives. In general, it is helpful to seek individuals who will bring pertinent knowledge and experience, but who also have different ways of looking at the issues at hand—in other words, people with potential for dissent. However, the underlying message of this book is not the *potential* differences that may come from diversity. The message is that real differences need expression—no matter what our demographic. In this way, the group is stimulated to consider and scrutinize alternatives and to come up with creative options.

Suppose that, in spite of all the reasons not to speak up, we do speak up. We have to be ready for the fact that group processes often conspire to limit our impact. Groups discuss what they share in common, not the unique information and position that you or I might bring to the table. They will give arguments in support of the preferred position—that is, their position. With dissent, however, they are less likely to become more extreme or to march to early consensus.

It Is *Not* About Arguing

There is a difficult distinction between arguing and debating. I find it interesting that the *Merriam-Webster* dictionary gives several definitions for the word "argue." These highlight the point I want to make. One definition is "to give reasons for or against something." Another is "to disagree or fight using angry words." The synonyms found in *Roget's Thesaurus* for "argue" include "disagree," "feud," "face off," and "sock it to." If you look at images of people in an argument, their heads are often projected forward, their mouths are open (at the same time), and one might be pointing a finger at the other. You can understand why some images show one person with her hands over her ears while this is going on. No one is listening.

The many news programs where people presumably debate are not much different. The guests often represent different points of view and come from different political parties. All their mouths are open at the same time as they interrupt one another and refute what they think the other is about to say. They are arguing, not discussing different points of view.

These different images show us that words are imprecise. Dissent provokes very different images. Many think immediately of someone who is ego-driven and likes to argue for the sake of argument. They think of dissent in terms of feuding and being an obstacle. In this book, we provide a different image: one of courage and conviction, one of robust discussion, one involving the energy and life of honest debate.

It Is *Not* About Contrivances

The value of dissent comes from the challenge it poses to consensus or the majority view. It liberates us to think for ourselves. It stimulates us to think anew—to search widely for information and possibilities. It stimulates divergent thinking.

Many accept the value of divergent thinking for good decision-making, and many accept the research showing the value of dissent. Yet they mistakenly interpret the proven value of dissent as a reason to place or to contrive opposition in a group. They assume that there is value in having an argument even if no one believes the counterposition. They thus use role-playing techniques or games in the hopes of achieving divergent thinking. As we have seen, role-playing does not have the stimulating effects of authentic dissent.

There is another reason why people applaud techniques like the devil's advocate: fundamentally, people want cohesion and harmony at all costs. I am convinced that the legacy of at least one popular guru of the past century has been the notion that we need to "get along"—that we need to win friends in order to influence. That's in fact the title of Dale Carnegie's book: *How to Win Friends and Influence People*. A timeless best-seller, it has sold over 15 million copies and is still running strong some eighty years after it was first published. A sample quote is: "The only way I can get you to do anything is by giving you what you want." This advice has merit in sales, but remember, Carnegie *was* a salesman. And he was good at it. He could sell you soap or bacon or courses in public speaking. His other lesson was: Be nice and Don't criticize.

I believe that the enormous and enduring success of Carnegie's book has contributed to the notion that nothing good happens unless we have harmony and liking. This assumption is deeply embedded in research traditions as well as in the popular mind. I believe it is also behind the desire to find techniques to stimulate more divergent thinking while preserving cohesion, liking, and harmony. The devil's advocate appears to fit the bill, but it is a contrived intellectual argument.

Most, but not all, of the research shows some value in the technique compared to having no challenge whatsoever.

Yet, as our own research has shown, the devil's advocate does not have the vigor or the stimulating qualities of authentic dissent. It may even stimulate the opposite of what we desire. It can increase thoughts that bolster initial beliefs.

I have another concern. It has always worried me when people think they have considered all sides of a position when in fact their thoughts have mostly attempted to bolster the position where they started. This was our finding with the devil's advocate. Perhaps my concerns arise because, for too many years, I have watched the pumped-up moral superiority by people who believe that they have considered all sides of an issue—and have no patience for any challenge to the position they have declared.

The easy message regarding contrived dissent is that those techniques don't work as well as authentic dissent. The more complicated message is that these techniques may have unintended negative consequences. Perhaps worse than thinking from a single perspective is the illusion that we have considered all sides.

WHAT THIS BOOK *IS* ABOUT

While half of this book shows the perils of consensus, the other half is more optimistic. I want to convince you that dissent has power and that it has value. So when we get annoyed and want to silence those who don't have power or numbers, I hope you will realize that we have much to learn from them. We especially have much to learn from those who think differently from us, the ones we might not seek as friends. We know what our friends and allies think. They think like us, and that makes us overconfident. That makes us more extreme, according to the research. Restricting our groups and teams to the like-minded doesn't make us good decision-makers.

I hope you remember that dissent brings two types of value: it breaks the power of consensus, enabling us to think more independently and to speak our own truth, and it stimulates our thinking. We become more inquiring, more divergent in our thinking, and more creative. Dissent is not just the presence of another position, but a stimulus to better and hopefully wiser thinking.

It *Is* About Authenticity and Conviction

Dissent has power. Most often we concentrate on the vulnerabilities of being the one who challenges the majority. Those vulnerabilities are real—but so is the power of a dissenting voice speaking with conviction, courage, and authenticity. That voice is clear, not a complicated contrivance.

That message came home to me quite recently when I attended a reception for Rise Up, a nonprofit organization founded by the sociologist Denise Dunning, whose mission is to advance health, education, and equity for girls, youth, and women everywhere. She doesn't pursue these goals by building schools or addressing small groups of girls, but by enabling girls and women to become advocates and change agents and transform their own lives and communities. They have accomplished some important legislative wins. The speaker at the reception was a young woman from Malawi, and what she had to say reminded me of the beauty of an authentic voice, one that challenges long-held cultural traditions and power.

> Her name was Memory Banda. Tiny and only eighteen years old, she delivered one of the most powerful talks I have heard in a long time. It wasn't the volume or even the tone of her voice. It was the message and the authenticity of that message. Her goal was to end child marriage.

Memory's own sister provided a powerful example and had motivated Memory to get involved in this movement. At the time, girls as young as ten would, by tradition, go to camps for sexual initiation. The "training" there was to learn how to please a man. There are men, termed the "hyenas," who would visit many girls across the country and teach them. Many of the girls became pregnant or developed HIV. When Memory's own sister, Mercy, became pregnant at the age of eleven, she was "married off" (not to the hyena, though). By age sixteen, she had three children. She was uneducated and had little hope for her future.

After encountering the Malawi Girls Empowerment Network, Memory started to get girls in her own village to speak up. They provided testimonials to reinforce the message: "I will marry when I want to." They provided a voice not previously heard, and they made it difficult to ignore the widespread practice of child marriage. Memory had started on her journey to change the law regarding child marriage. Five years later, it would be a reality.

In February 2015, Malawi raised the legal age of marriage from fifteen to eighteen. This was no small accomplishment given that Malawi has one of the highest rates of child marriage in the world—girls as young as nine had been married off. The route to success was similar to the successful campaign in Liberia. They started by convincing local chieftains that girls needed education and learned to leverage the power of that cause to legislators.

Memory had already been a rogue, a rebel. She had refused to go to the mandated camp, even though she undoubtedly faced a great deal of pressure from her community. Girls were expected to do what they were told and to remain quiet even if it was painful. Memory said "NO." When her sister became a victim of the then-current laws, she became active, joining a small band of activist girls who were able to get the law changed.

These were big wins in Malawi considering the culture and history of child marriage there. They underscore some of the principles detailed throughout this book. These girls embodied the principles of consistency and persistence. They were full of conviction. They didn't parse their words or compromise. They stood up to family and community pressure. They engaged tribal leaders. They appeared before legislative bodies. Their voices had power.

It *Is* About Speaking Up

Many of us are constantly concerned about what we should say and how we should say it. We worry about not offending, about being effective, and we ponder the trade-offs between self-interested strategy and doing the right thing. We feel that we don't have the right to speak freely, in spite of our treasured First Amendment in this country. These feelings of constraint hold whether we are high or low on the totem pole, whether we come from favored or less favored categories. We rarely have the luxury of speaking up without analyzing the likely consequences.

Speaking the truth does not mean being rude or disrespectful. It does not mean malevolent intentions to harm or denigrate someone. Speaking up is when you have a position that you believe to be true. This is the image of the dissenter in this book.

We need dissent. I for one love the university when it truly is a forum for opposing viewpoints. A dissenting view is energizing and clarifying. Listening to a dissenting view makes us less likely to live in an ideological bubble. It liberates us to think on our own and to share the truth, as we best see it. Dissent encourages us to search, to think, and to evolve in our understanding.

Whether at universities or in companies or in chats at cafés, we have been waiting to exhale. Honest discourse is in too short a supply. One way for us to have that honest discourse is to be curious, to embrace ideas different from our own. It is hard to offend when you have good intentions and respect for the other.

It *Is* About Protecting Different Views

This of course is the heart of the book: the optimistic findings that our thinking is stimulated by dissent—authentic dissent. And as previously discussed, we must distinguish dissent from diversity. It is not the presence of demographic diversity, nor even just the presence of opinion diversity, that favors good decision-making. It is challenge. When competing and authentically held views are expressed, our thinking and decision-making benefit.

As we manage groups and organizations, it is important that we select individuals who not only have pertinent knowledge and experience but also are likely to look at issues from a different perspective. However, we cannot underestimate the culture of the group or the organization. I have written elsewhere on the topic of corporate cultures for innovation; here I would say that, minimally, people need to feel safe in expressing dissent in a group. It is even better if they feel that dissent is welcomed. Such a group has a chance to become a "hot group" known for its synergy and high levels of creativity.

Jane Wales, CEO of the World Affairs Council, has tried to put these principles into practice. She has a remarkable biography, having served as deputy assistant secretary of state under President Jimmy Carter and as a special assistant to President Bill Clinton. My interview with her was one of the more thoughtful discussions I have had in a long time.

With her wide-ranging experience and head-spinning knowledge of world affairs, Wales brings the perspective of real-life decisions. She is keenly aware of how emotions and bias in many forms rule most policy decisions, making it difficult to convince people of what is in everyone's interest. In describing these issues, Wales recognizes the importance of being open to change, though at the same time she knows that we never quite get it right.

Her mission was to modernize the World Affairs Council, which meant updating a model that had been in place since 1948. As CEO, she put several strategic planning processes in place. One was dominated by the senior team and longtime members of the board. For another, she systematically engaged the full staff as well as newer members of the board. Her goal was to ensure that all voices were heard.

Her message was: Let's be extreme. Let's not tinker at the edges or make incremental changes. If the World Affairs Council were a media company, how would we structure it, what would be our products, and how would we deliver them? If our goal were to build a community, what would we look like? If we were producing conferences, what would we look like?

The message was loud and clear: the World Affairs Council was going to be different. They would work as teams. They were going to be different. Whatever changes were needed, they should and would do. What she found was that her board was energized and her staff was engaged. Before, the model was to deliver messages on-site and in person to a passive audience who sat still and listened. Now they would use broadcasting and online media and aim for greater audience engagement. Instead of using a lecture format, people interacted. Their views were elicited. Jane made the World Affairs Council a place where new ideas were safe. More than that, she welcomed them.

It *Is* About Debate, Not Harmony

Dale Carnegie advised that we be nice and, above all, not criticize each other. If we criticize others, we won't make the sale. This may be true for making the sale, but it's not true for groups that want to make good decisions and find creative solutions. When it comes to creativity, the message should be that ideas are welcome and the more novel the better. Yet it is interesting to see that consultants often follow the Carnegie prescriptions instead.

A similar message was conveyed by Alex Osborn, who gave us the four brainstorming rules, one of which was "do not criticize." He argued that criticism would shut people down and reduce creative idea generation. This notion may be intuitively plausible, but as studies in the United States and France have confirmed, the freedom to criticize *aids* rather than impedes the generation of ideas.

It always struck me that rules like "do not criticize" suggest that we are so fragile and tender that we can't tolerate someone suggesting that there is a flaw in our thinking or that there is a better idea. Such rules also seem to distract focus from the issue at hand—that issue being to generate ideas that solve the problem. It is hard to freewheel when you are worried about what you say and how you say it. The research shows that debate, even criticism, can be a boon to brainstorming.

NOT A ROSE GARDEN, BUT THERE ARE ROSES

The emphasis of this book is not to *create* dissent but to *permit* it—even to *welcome* dissent if it is authentic. People belonging to strong research groups and the "hot groups" found in many start-ups thrive on differing views. If you look back to the most successful team project you have ever worked on, it almost surely was one with high energy, a combat of ideas, and an excitement of building on each other's ideas. Dialogue and debate can be invigorating. We learn and reassess.

The big problem, it seems to me, is the suppression of dissent. Paraphrasing John Stuart Mill, when dissent is suppressed, the group and organization suffer. If the dissent is correct, the group is deprived of a truth, and if it is wrong, the group is deprived of the stimulation for thought. With consensus, our minds go on automatic pilot. Our fears about speaking up sometimes lead us to turn a blind eye to bad decisions or ethical violations.

There may be reasonable calculations to be made about whether or not to speak up; nevertheless, the fear of speaking up can create major problems in organizations. We see the effects in scandals such as the rogue trader known as "the London Whale" losing at least $6.2 billion for JPMorgan Chase in 2012 by doubling down on his bets. But it was not just one individual who stoked that scandal; also playing a part was the complicity of other traders, some of whom kept two separate books to minimize the size of the losses. There were undoubtedly many others who remained silent about what they suspected or knew. After all, risk limits were breached more than three hundred times. We saw it in the classic example of groupthink— the disastrous Bay of Pigs decision. Arthur Schlesinger opposed it, but he remained silent—and later reproached himself for not speaking up. We also see the effects of not speaking up in situations closer to home. When everyone is "on board," we keep silent. It is easier—and safer—to hide behind what everyone else is doing. It is easier "to go along and to get along." Who wants to be a martyr?

The optimism for dissent, however, is also very real. We see more people seriously inviting and even embracing diversity of viewpoints—several of them were highlighted in this book. We see more CEOs and managers who are sufficiently confident to make dissent safe in their organizations. They welcome differing views, for they realize their value, both personally and financially. Some of the best entrepreneurs challenge themselves continuously. Scott Cook, founder of Intuit, for example, repeatedly tries to beat himself. David Teece, CEO of Berkeley Research Group, has a similar mentality. He is unafraid of challenge; in fact, he invites it. Some of the best doctors make a practice of seeking the opinions of other specialists. In San Francisco, physicians Jacob Johnson and Jesse Dohemann, for example, regularly seek input that will challenge or revise their own diagnoses.

THE TAKE-HOME

Rather than worry about appeasing others or making sure we do not offend by disagreeing with them, the message of this book is that there is importance and value in authentic debate. The idea that dissent causes irritation and conflict is only partially accurate. Dissent and debate also bring joy and invigorate discussion. Best of all, genuine dissent and debate not only make us think but make us think well. We become free to "know what we know." We make better decisions, find more creative solutions, and are better able to render justice.

I will let the philosopher Eric Hoffer bring this book to its close beautifully and succinctly: "The beginning of thought is in disagreement—not only with others but also with ourselves."

NOTES

INTRODUCTION

3   **Three days before Christmas, in 1978:** National Transportation Safety Board (NTSB), "Aircraft Accident Report: United Air Lines, Inc., McDonnell-Douglas DC-8–61, N8082U, Portland, Oregon, December 28, 1978," NTSB-AAR-79–7 (Washington, DC: NTSB, June 7, 1979), www.ntsb.gov/investigations /AccidentReports/Reports/AAR7907.pdf.

4   **twenty-three people were seriously injured:** Ibid., 23.

5   **Perhaps the stress prevented them from noticing:** James A. Easterbrook, "The Effect of Emotion on Cue Utilization and the Organization of Behavior," *Psychological Review* 66, no. 3 (1959): 183–201. See generally Jonathan Fawcett, Evan Risko, and Alan Kingstone, eds., *The Handbook of Attention* (Cambridge, MA: MIT Press, 2015).

6   **"three [3,000 pounds] on the fuel and that's it":** NTSB, "Aircraft Accident Report," 6.

6   "About four thousand, well, make it three thousand": Ibid., 7.
6   "I think you just lost number four": Ibid.
6   "Why?" asked the captain: Ibid.
6   "Fuel," said the first officer: Ibid.
6   "Portland tower, United one seventy three heavy": Ibid., 9.
6   At the crash site, however: Ibid.
7   Even then, we know that people do not always follow the truth:
     Charlan Jeanne Nemeth and Joel Wachtler, "Creative Problem
     Solving as a Result of Majority vs. Minority Influence," *European
     Journal of Social Psychology* 13, no. 1 (1983): 45–55.
8   Whether it is in an organization or a start-up: Dacher Keltner,
     Deborah Gruenfeld, and Cameron Anderson, "Power, Approach,
     and Inhibition," *Psychological Review* 110 (2001): 265–284.
10 This book also serves as a counter to books: James Charles
     Collins and Jerry I. Porras, *Built to Last: Successful Habits of
     Visionary Companies* (New York: HarperCollins, 2002).
10 "that people have upon the beliefs or behavior of others": Elliot
     Aronson, *The Social Animal* (New York: Macmillan, 2003), 6.
10 many in the field still view it as unlikely: Bibb Latané and
     Sharon Wolf, "The Social Impact of Majorities and Minorities,"
     Psychological Review 88, no. 5 (1981): 438.
11 Reducing the broad area of social influence to persuasion:
     Robert B. Cialdini, *Influence: The Psychology of Persuasion* (New
     York: Morrow, 1993).
11 what most researchers consider good decision-making: Irving
     L. Janis and Leon Mann, *Decision Making: A Psychological Anal-
     ysis of Conflict, Choice, and Commitment* (New York: Free Press,
     1977).
15 the nail that sticks up will be hammered down: "Learn Jap-
     anese: 30 Japanese Proverbs & Sayings. Part 2," Linguajunkie
     .com, www.linguajunkie.com/japanese/learn-japanese-proverbs
     -sayings (accessed December 10, 2016).
19 "We must learn to welcome": J. William Fulbright, speech deliv-
     ered before the US Senate, Washington, DC, March 27, 1964.
20 "Whenever you find that you are on the side of the majority":
     Mark Twain, *Mark Twain's Notebook* (New York: Harper and
     Brothers, 1909), 393.

CHAPTER 1: NUMBERS RULE

23   **One segment from 1962:** Allen Funt and Philip G. Zimbardo, "Face the Rear," in *Candid Camera Classics for Teaching Social Psychology* (video) (Boston: McGraw-Hill Films, 1992).

24   **The jury may take hours or days to reach a verdict:** Harry Kalven Jr. and Hans Zeisel, *The American Jury* (Boston: Little, Brown, 1966).

25   **My colleagues and I have found that people:** Charlan Nemeth and Cynthia Chiles, "Modelling Courage: The Role of Dissent in Fostering Independence," *European Journal of Social Psychology* 18, no. 3 (1988): 275–280.

26   **best-sellers such as *The Wisdom of Crowds* inadvertently reinforce:** James Surowiecki, *The Wisdom of Crowds: Why the Many Are Smarter Than the Few and How Collective Wisdom Shapes Business, Economies, Societies, and Nations* (New York: Doubleday, 2004).

27   **The classic study of this phenomenon was conducted:** Solomon E. Asch, "Studies of Independence and Conformity: I. A Minority of One Against a Unanimous Majority," *Psychological Monographs: General and Applied* 70, no. 9 (1956): 1–70.

28   **This study, while first conducted half a century ago:** Rob Bond and Peter B. Smith, "Culture and Conformity: A Meta-Analysis of Studies Using Asch's (1952b, 1956) Line Judgment Task," *Psychological Bulletin* 119, no. 1 (1996): 111–137.

28   **The amount of conformity:** Aronson, *The Social Animal*; Asch, "Studies of Independence and Conformity."

29   **"Fifty million Frenchmen can't be wrong":** Fred Fisher, Billy Rose, William Raskin, and Jack Kaufman "Fifty Million Frenchmen Can't Be Wrong" (Orange, NJ: Edison, 1927).

29   **Many people can relate to the Japanese proverb:** Roy F. Baumeister and Brad J. Bushman, *Social Psychology and Human Nature* (Belmont, CA: Thomson Learning, 2008).

29   **In the early study by Asch:** Asch, "Studies of Independence and Conformity."

31   **Some one hundred studies have investigated:** Bond and Smith, "Culture and Conformity."

31	More importantly, they feared rejection: Baumeister and Bush-man, *Social Psychology.*

31	that fear may be an even more potent reason: David S. Wallace, Rene M. Paulson, Charles G. Lord, and Charles F. Bond Jr., "Which Behaviors Do Attitudes Predict? Meta-analyzing the Effects of Social Pressure and Perceived Difficulty," *Review of General Psychology* 9, no. 3 (2005): 214–227.

31	When we are motivated to believe that the majority: Ziva Kunda, "The Case for Motivated Reasoning," *Psychological Bulletin* 108, no. 3 (1990): 480–498.

31	Empirical work by economists confirms: Abhijit V. Banerjee, "A Simple Model of Herd Behavior," *Quarterly Journal of Economics* (1992): 797–817.

31	Between 1995 and 2000, the NASDAQ: "2001 Nasdaq 100 Historical Prices/Charts," FuturesTradingCharts.com, http://futures.tradingcharts.com/historical/ND/2001/0/continuous.html (accessed November 14, 2015).

31	bubbles are not necessarily evidence: Robert J. Shiller, "How a Bubble Stayed Under the Radar," *New York Times,* March 2, 2008.

32	"reputational calculation": John Maynard Keynes, *The General Theory of Employment, Interest, and Money* (New York: Harcourt, Brace, 1936).

32	around 70 percent of employees don't speak up: Kathleen D. Ryan and Daniel K. Oestreich, *Driving Fear Out of the Workplace: How to Overcome the Invisible Barriers to Quality, Productivity, and Innovation* (San Francisco: Jossey-Bass, 1991).

32	We see similar kinds of following in consumer behavior: Nan Hu, Ling Liu, and Jie Jennifer Zhang, "Do Online Reviews Affect Product Sales? The Role of Reviewer Characteristics and Temporal Effects," *Information Technology and Management* 9, no. 3 (2008): 201–214.

33	A number of businesses capitalize: Jen-Hung Huang and Yi-Fen Chen, "Herding in Online Product Choice," *Psychology and Marketing* 23, no. 5 (2006): 413–428.

33	A listed business with a majority of good ratings: Michael Luca, "Reviews, Reputation, and Revenue: The Case of Yelp.com,"

Harvard Business School Working Paper 12–016, September 16, 2011.

33 **The Holy Grail of book recommendations:** Alan T. Sorensen, "Bestseller Lists and Product Variety," *Journal of Industrial Economics* 55, no. 4 (2007): 715–738.

34 **"almost 75 percent of guests who are asked to participate":** Noah J. Goldstein, Robert B. Cialdini, and Vladas Griskevicius, "A Room with a Viewpoint: Using Social Norms to Motivate Environmental Conservation in Hotels," *Journal of Consumer Research* 35, no. 3 (2008): 472.

34 **"People start pollution. People can stop pollution":** "Pollution: Keep America Beautiful—Iron Eyes Cody," *Ad Council*, www .adcouncil.org/Our-Work/The-Classics/Pollution-Keep -America-Beautiful-Iron-Eyes-Cody.

34 **it was named one of the top one hundred advertising campaigns:** "Ad Age Advertising Century: Top 100 Campaigns," *AdvertisingAge*, March 29, 1999, http://adage.com/article/special -report-the-advertising-century/ad-age-advertising-century -top-100-advertising-campaigns/140150/.

35 **this message might not have had its intended effect:** Robert B. Cialdini, Linda J. Demaine, Brad J. Sagarin, Daniel W. Barrett, Kelton Rhaods, and Patricia L. Winters, "Managing Social Norms for Persuasive Impact," *Social Influence* 1, no. 1 (2006): 3–15.

36 **There are many books and articles:** For an overview, see Surowiecki, *The Wisdom of Crowds.*

37 **One specific way to reduce that fear is through anonymity:** John C. Turner, *Social Influence* (Bristol, PA: Thomson Brooks/ Cole Publishing Co, 1991); Morton Deutsch and Harold B. Gerard, "A Study of Normative and Informational Social Influences upon Individual Judgment," *Journal of Abnormal and Social Psychology* 51, no. 3 (1955): 629–636.

37 **interacting over networked computers rather than face to face:** Shirley S. Ho and Douglas M. McLeod, "Social-Psychological Influences on Opinion Expression in Face-to-Face and Computer-Mediated Communication," *Communication Research* 35, no. 2 (2008): 190–207.

CHAPTER 2: EVEN ONE DISSENTER MAKES A DIFFERENCE

40   **one way is through anonymity:** Morton Deutsch and Harold B. Gerard, "A Study of Normative and Informational Social Influences upon Individual Judgment," *Journal of Abnormal and Social Psychology* 51, no. 3 (1955): 629–636.

41   **One early and interesting study:** Ibid.

43   **Asch's early length-of-lines study:** Solomon E. Asch, "Opinions and Social Pressure," *Scientific American* 193 (1955): 31–35.

43   **the evidence shows that, even here:** Vernon L. Allen and John M. Levine, "Social Support, Dissent, and Conformity," *Sociometry* 31, no. 2 (1968): 138–149.

44   **agreement with the erroneous majority dropped:** Ibid.

44   **we know that people fear being that "one":** Charlan Jeanne Nemeth and Brendan Nemeth-Brown, "Better Than Individuals? The Potential Benefits of Dissent and Diversity for Group Creativity," in *Group Creativity: Innovation Through Collaboration*, edited by Paul Paulus and Bernard Nijstad, 63–84 (Oxford: Oxford University Press, 2003).

45   **In a now-classic experiment:** Stanley Schachter, "Deviation, Rejection, and Communication," *Journal of Abnormal and Social Psychology* 46, no. 2 (1951): 190–207.

47   **The majority will try to convince the dissenter:** Ibid.

48   **We looked at this possibility in one of our own studies:** Nemeth and Chiles, "Modelling Courage."

CHAPTER 3: DISSENT AS AN ART
IN CHANGING HEARTS AND MINDS

52   **Being the target of most of the communication:** Schachter, "Deviation, Rejection, and Communication."

52   **It took two centuries for the ban:** Douglas O. Linder, "The Trial of Galileo: A Chronology," *Famous Trials*, http://law2.umkc.edu /faculty/projects/ftrials/galileo/galileochronology.html.

53   **He was ridiculed, not permitted to speak:** Ernest Jones, *The Life and Work of Sigmund Freud* (New York: Basic Books, 1961), 299.

53   **Some attributed his theories:** E. M. Thornton, *Freud and Cocaine: The Freudian Fallacy* (London: Blond & Briggs, 1983).

53   Concepts like the unconscious or repression: John F. Kilh-
     strom, "Is Freud Still Alive? No, Not Really," in *Hilgard's In-
     troduction to Psychology*, 13th ed., edited by Rita L. Atkinson,
     Richard C. Atkinson, Edward E. Smith, Daryl J. Bem, and Su-
     san Nolen-Hoeksema (New York: Harcourt Brace Jovanovich,
     1999).

53   Think of Jeffrey Wigand: *The Insider*, directed by Michael Mann
     (Burbank, CA: Touchstone Pictures, 1999).

54   Glenn Greenwald, a journalist with *The Guardian* newspaper:
     Glenn Greenwald, "NSA Collecting Phone Records of Millions
     of Verizon Customers Daily," *Guardian*, June 6, 2013.

54   PRISM, a seven-year NSA data mining program: Glenn
     Greenwald and Ewen MacAskill, "NSA Prism Program Taps
     in to User Data of Apple, Google, and Others," *The Guardian*,
     June 7, 2013.

54   a "balance" of security and privacy: "Edward Snowden: Time-
     line," *BBC News*, August 20, 2013, www.bbc.co.uk/news/world
     -us-canada-23768248; Andrew Serwin, "Striking the Balance—
     Privacy versus Security and the New White House Report,"
     Privacy Advisor, December 19, 2013; https://iapp.org/news/a
     /striking-the-balanceprivacy-versus-security-and-the-new-white
     -house-report/

54   The *Guardian* disclosed that he was Edward Snowden: Al-
     ana Horowitz, "Booz Allen Hamilton: Edward Snowden News
     'Shocking,' 'A Grave Violation,'" *Huffington Post*, June 10, 2013,
     www.huffingtonpost.com/2013/06/09/booz-allen-hamilton
     -edward-snowden-nsa_n_3412609.html.

55   "Mr. Snowden told the truth in the name of privacy": Phil
     Black, Matt Smith, and Catherine E. Shoichet, "Snowden on
     the Run, Seeks Asylum in Ecuador," *CNN*, June 24, 2013, www
     .cnn.com/2013/06/23/politics/nsa-leaks/.

55   Snowden had "no intention of hiding": Ashley Fantz, "NSA
     Leaker Ignites Global Debate: Hero or Traitor?" *CNN*, June 10,
     2013, www.cnn.com/2013/06/10/us/snowden-leaker-reaction/.

55   "The NSA has built an infrastructure": Ewen MacAskill, "Ed-
     ward Snowden, NSA Files Source: 'If They Want to Get You, in
     Time They Will,'" *The Guardian*, June 10, 2013.

55   **Those in the hero camp saw him as a man:** Hadas Gold, "Daniel Ellsberg Thanks Edward Snowden," *Politico,* June 10, 2013, www.politico.com/story/2013/06/daniel-ellsberg-edward -snowden-nsa-leak-92478.html.

55   **He was variously described as "arrogant":** David Auerbach, "I Would Have Hired Edward Snowden," *Slate,* June 18, 2013, www.slate.com/articles/technology/technology/2013/06/i _would_have_hired_nsa_whistleblower_edward_snowden .html; David Brooks, "The Solitary Leaker," *New York Times,* June 10, 2013; Eric Niiler, "The Bean-Spillers: Why Do They Leak?" *Seeker,* June 10, 2013, www.seeker.com/the-bean-spillers -why-do-they-leak-1767586613.html.

55   **"impossibly self-important":** Ralph Peters, "Making Treason Cool," *New York Post,* June 11, 2013.

56   **He now had no travel documents:** "US Officials Fume over Russia Granting Asylum to Snowden," *Fox News,* August 1, 2013, www.foxnews.com/politics/2013/08/01/snowden-reportedly -leaves-moscow-airport-enters-russia-on-refugee-status/.

56   **One country after another:** Michael Pearson, Matt Smith, and Jethro Mullen, "Snowden's Asylum Options Dwindle," *CNN,* July 2, 2013, www.cnn.com/2013/07/02/politics/nsa-leak/.

56   **Eventually, Russian president Vladimir Putin:** Ilya Arkhipov and Olga Tanas, "Putin Shows Global Mojo to Russians as US Fumes over Snowden," *Bloomberg,* August 1, 2013, available to subscribers at: www.bloomberg.com/news/2013-08-01 /putin-shows-global-mojo-to-russians-as-u-s-fumes-over -snowden.html.

57   **Not only had the reaction been worldwide:** Brian Stelter, "NSA: The Story of the Summer" (interview with Glenn Greenwald), *CNN: Reliable Sources,* September 1, 2013, www.cnn.com /videos/bestoftv/2013/09/01/rs-nsa-the-story-of-the-summer .cnn.

57   **A federal appeals court ruled:** Devlin Barrett and Damian Paletta, "NSA Phone Program Is Illegal, Appeals Court Rules," *Wall Street Journal,* May 7, 2015.

58   **"unwarranted government surveillance":** Jim Stavridis and Dave Weinstein, "Apple vs. FBI Is Not About Privacy vs. Security—It's

About How to Achieve Both," *Huffington Post*, March 8, 2016, www.huffingtonpost.com/admiral-jim-stavridis-ret/apple -fbi-privacy-security_b_9404314.html.

58   **The first experimental study of how dissenters:** Serge Moscovici, E. Lage, and M. Naffrechoux, "Influence of a Consistent Minority on the Responses of a Majority in a Color Perception Task," *Sociometry* 32, no. 4 (1969): 365–380.

61   **subsequent research has repeatedly replicated:** Charlan J. Nemeth, "Minority Influence Theory," in *Handbook of Theories of Social Psychology*, vol. 2, edited by Paul A. M. Van Lange, Arie W. Kruglanski, and E. Tory Higgins (Thousand Oaks, CA: Sage Publications, 2011), 362–378.

61   **without consistency, a minority voice does not persuade:** Miles Hewstone and Robin Martin, "Minority Influence: From Groups to Attitudes and Back Again," in *Minority Influence and Innovation: Antecedents, Processes, and Consequences*, edited by Robin Martin and Miles Hewstone (New York: Psychology Press, 2010), 365–394.

61   **fewer than 5 percent of verdicts are the position:** Kalven and Zeisel, *The American Jury*.

61   **In our own experimental studies using mock-jury deliberations:** Charlan Nemeth, "Interactions Between Jurors as a Function of Majority vs. Unanimity Decision Rules," *Journal of Applied Social Psychology* 7, no. 1 (1977): 38–56.

62   **dissenters change more minds in private than in public:** Martin and Hewstone, *Minority Influence and Innovation*.

62   **In their private judgments of that case:** Charlan Nemeth and Joel Wachtler, "Creating Perceptions of Consistency and Confidence: A Necessary Condition for Minority Influence," *Sociometry* 37 (1974): 529–540.

63   **A dissenter can become more artful in articulating:** Charlan Nemeth, Mark Swedlund, and Barbara Kanki, "Patterning of the Minority's Responses and Their Influence on the Majority," *European Journal of Social Psychology* 4 (1974): 53–64.

63   **He was in fact advised to compromise:** Helen W. Puner, *Sigmund Freud: His Life and Mind* (New Brunswick, NJ: Transaction Publishers, 1992).

63   **what about the extensive research supporting the common advice:** Seungwoo Kwon and Laurie R. Weingart, "Unilateral Concessions from the Other Party: Concession Behavior, Attributions, and Negotiation Judgments," *Journal of Applied Psychology* 89, no. 2 (2004): 263.

64   **and scores of studies suggest that it is:** Martin and Hewstone, *Minority Influence and Innovation;* Nemeth, "Minority Influence Theory."

64   **You may be thinking that it is all fine and good:** Jeffrey Z. Rubin and Bert R. Brown, *The Social Psychology of Bargaining and Negotiation* (New York: Academic Press, 1975).

65   **Negotiation research argues for the power:** Rubin and Brown, *Bargaining and Negotiation;* Leigh Thompson, *The Truth About Negotiations* (Upper Saddle River, NJ: Pearson Education, 2013).

65   **The other line of research:** Gabriel Mugny and Stamos Papastamou, *The Power of Minorities* (London: Academic Press, 1982).

66   **one individual took a minority position:** Charlan Nemeth and Alice G. Brilmayer, "Negotiation Versus Influence," *European Journal of Social Psychology* 17, no. 1 (1987): 45–56.

68   **dissenters have "hidden" influence:** Gabriel Mugny and Juan A. Perez, *The Social Psychology of Minority Influence* (Cambridge: Cambridge University Press, 1991); John M. Levine and Radmila Prislin, "Majority and Minority Influence," in *Group Processes*, edited by John M. Levine (New York: Routledge, 2013), 135–164; William D. Crano, *The Rules of Influence: Winning When You're in the Minority* (New York: St. Martin's Press, 2012).

68   **We see this pattern in many of our studies:** Nemeth, "Minority Influence Theory."

71   **It takes time and a choreography:** Gabriel Mugny and Stamos Papastamou, "When Rigidity Does Not Fail: Individualization and Psychologization as Resistances to the Diffusion of Minority Innovations," *European Journal of Social Psychology* (1980): 10, 43–61.

71   **The choreography of the dissenter's verbal:** For further reviews, see Hewstone and Martin, "Minority Influence"; Mugny and Perez, *The Social Psychology of Minority Influence.*

71 Some elements of this choreography: *Twelve Angry Men*, directed by Sidney Lumet (Beverly Hills, CA: MGM Studios, 1957).

78 Snowden had performed a "public service": Eyder Peralta, "Former AG Holder Says Edward Snowden's Leak Was a 'Public Service,'" *NPR*, May 31, 2016, www.npr.org/sections/thetwo -way/2016/05/31/480179898/former-ag-holder-says-edward -snowdens-leak-was-a-public-service.

CHAPTER 4: CONSENSUS NARROWS THINKING— AND KILLS RATIONALITY

82 We have many biases in how we select and interpret: Dieter Frey, "Recent Research on Selective Exposure to Information," *Advances in Experimental Social Psychology* 19 (1986): 41–80.

83 On November 19, 1978, many people awoke to the news: Jennifer Rosenberg, "The Jonestown Massacre," *ThoughtCo*, February 6, 2017, http://history1900s.about.com/od/1970s/p /jonestown.htm.

83 The evidence is that these people committed mass suicide: Rick Paulas, "The Unanswerable Questions of Jonestown," *Pacific Standard*, October 20, 2015, www.psmag.com/politics-and -law/the-unanswerable-questions-of-jonestown.

85 Children, for example, might be beaten in public: Jeannie Mills, *Six Years with God: Life Inside Rev. Jim Jones's Peoples Temple* New York: A&W Publishers (1979).

85 Jim Jones's notion of a spiritual ideal: Catherine B. Abbott, "Selling Jonestown: Religion, Socialism, and Revolutionary Suicide in Peoples Temple," *Alternative Considerations of Jonestown & Peoples Temple*, August 19, 2014, http://jonestown.sdsu.edu /?page_id=30863.

85 He represented California's Eleventh District: Justin Peters, "The Forgotten, Non-Kool-Aid-Drinking Victims of the Jonestown Massacre," *Slate*, November 18, 2013, www.slate.com/blogs /crime/2013/11/18/leo_ryan_jonestown_the_forgotten_non _kool_aid_drinking_victims_of_the_jonestown.html.

86 After they arrived at the compound: Ibid.

86   **Someone passed a note:** Staff Investigative Group, *The Assassination of Representative Leo J. Ryan and the Jonestown, Guyana Tragedy: Report of a Staff Investigative Group to the Committee on Foreign Affairs, US House of Representatives*, 96th Cong., 1st sess., House Document 96–223, May 15, 1979, 4, http://jonestown.sdsu.edu/?page_id=13674.

86   **He died of a bullet wound to the head:** "Guyana Inquest— Interview of Odell Rhodes," *Alternative Considerations of Jonestown & Peoples Temple*, http://jonestown.sdsu.edu/wp-content/uploads/2013/10/GuyanaInquest.pdf.

87   **As John Stuart Mill recognized:** Charlan Jeanne Nemeth, "Dissent, Group Process, and Creativity: The Contribution of Minority Influence," in *Advances in Group Processes*, vol. 2, edited by Edward Lawler, 57–75 (Greenwich, CT: JAI Press, 1985), 57–75.

87   **There is a reason why cultlike organizations:** Collins and Porras, *Built to Last*.

88   **Similar stories are told about Scientology:** Lawrence Wright, *Going Clear: Scientology, Hollywood, and the Prison of Belief* (New York: Vintage Books, 2013).

89   **When everyone in the room laughs:** Robert R. Provine, "Contagious Laughter: Laughter Is a Sufficient Stimulus for Laughs and Smiles," *Bulletin of the Psychonomic Society* (1992): 30, 1–4.

90   **A study that we conducted at UC Berkeley:** Charlan J. Nemeth and John Rogers, "Dissent and the Search for Information," *British Journal of Social Psychology* 35, no. 1 (1996): 67–76.

94   **The task involved anagram solutions:** Charlan J. Nemeth and Julianne L. Kwan, "Minority Influence, Divergent Thinking, and Detection of Correct Solutions," *Journal of Applied Social Psychology* 17, no. 9 (1987): 788–799.

97   **One study demonstrates this tendency to not "see" solutions:** Charlan J. Nemeth and Joel Wachtler, "Creative Problem Solving as a Result of Majority vs. Minority Influence," *European Journal of Social Psychology* 13, no. 1 (1983): 45–55.

98   **This may be one reason for the tragedy:** NTSB, "Aircraft Accident Report."

99   **They crashed in a suburb of Portland only six nautical miles:** Ibid.

100   **In summary, the NTSB observed that the captain:** Ibid., 1.

100   **it was a cockpit variant:** "The only thing necessary for the triumph of evil is for good men to do nothing" is often attributed to Edmund Burke, who said something along these lines in his essay "Thoughts on the Cause of the Present Discontents."

100   **The NTSB recognized that the crew may have conformed:** NTSB, "Aircraft Accident Report," 27.

101   **The NTSB's preferred solution:** Ibid., 30.

101   **it is not very effective in combating biases:** Daniel Kahneman, *Thinking, Fast and Slow* (New York: Macmillan, 2011).

101   **one of our studies investigated the originality of thought:** Charlan J. Nemeth and Julianne L. Kwan, "Originality of Word Associations as a Function of Majority vs. Minority Influence," *Social Psychology Quarterly* 48, no. 3 (1985): 277–282.

102   **In a study testing the potential advantages:** Charlan Nemeth, Kathleen Mosier, and Cyntia Chiles, "When Convergent Thought Improves Performance: Majority vs. Minority Influence," *Personality and Social Psychology Bulletin* 18 (1992): 139–144.

102   **it is called the Stroop test:** J. Ridley Stroop, "Studies of Interference in Serial Verbal Reactions," *Journal of Experimental Psychology* 18 (1935): 643–662.

103   **the focus of a majority judgment was varied:** Nemeth, Mosier, and Chiles, "When Convergent Thought Improves Performance."

CHAPTER 5: DISSENT DIVERSIFIES— AND STRENGTHENS THINKING

107   **An antidote was already apparent:** Asch, "Opinions and Social Pressure."

108   **It was one-third lower than when no ally was present:** Vernon L. Allen and John M. Levine, "Social Support and Conformity: The Role of Independent Assessment of Reality," *Journal of Experimental Social Psychology* 7, no. 1 (1971): 48–58.

110   **not all American juries are required to deliberate to unanimity:** Apodaca v. Oregon, 406 US 404 (1972); Johnson v. Louisiana, 406 US 356 (1972).

110   **While a professor at the University of Virginia:** In fact, I had decided against becoming an attorney, since I was female and

women didn't practice before the bar in those days. They generally did research for a male lawyer.

110   **the greatest group of four undergraduates:** Edward Hodge, Patrick Huyghe, David Doggett, and John Sullivan.

110   **but the real insight came from repeatedly watching:** Charlan Nemeth, "Rules Governing Jury Deliberations: A Consideration of Recent Changes," in *Psychology and the Law: Research Frontiers*, edited by Gordon Bermant, Charlan Nemeth, and Neil Vidmar (Lexington, MA: D. C. Heath & Co./Lexington Books, 1976); Nemeth, "Interactions Between Jurors."

111   **That insight took hold:** Much credit is due to two graduate students, Jeff Endicott and Joel Wachtler, who came with me from Chicago to Virginia. The discussions and research with them made an important contribution.

112   **We favor information that confirms our own beliefs:** Leon Festinger, *A Theory of Cognitive Dissonance* (Row, Peterson and Co., 1957); William Hart, Dolores Albarracín, Alice H. Eagly, Inge Brechan, Matthew J. Lindberg, and Lisa Merrill, "Feeling Validated Versus Being Correct: A Meta-Analysis of Selective Exposure to Information," *Psychological Bulletin* 135, no. 4 (2009): 555–588.

112   **university students were given the results of a survey:** Nemeth and Rogers, "Dissent and the Search for Information."

113   **In one, this involved recall of information:** Charlan Nemeth, Ofra Mayseless, Jeffrey Sherman, and Yvonne Brown, "Exposure to Dissent and Recall of Information," *Journal of Personality and Social Psychology* 58, no. 3 (1990): 429–437.

115   **Much like the research on persuasion:** Nemeth and Brilmayer, "Negotiation Versus Influence."

115   **Adding to the evidence that dissent stimulates attention:** Nemeth and Wachtler, "Creative Problem Solving."

116   **reconsider another study briefly described:** Nemeth and Kwan, "Minority Influence, Divergent Thinking."

120   **When he released the classified documents:** Greenwald, "NSA Collecting Phone Records of Millions."

120   **there was some evidence that he changed minds:** Barrett and Paletta, "NSA Phone Program Is Illegal."

120   **President Obama, who had vigorously defended:** Steven Nelson, "Senate Passes Freedom Act, Ending Patriot Act Provision Lapse," *U.S. News & World Report*, June 2, 2015.

121   **the Church Committee, which had warned us:** Cindy Cohn and Trevor Timm, "In Response to the NSA, We Need a New Church Committee and We Need It Now," *Electronic Frontier Foundation*, June 7, 2013, www.eff.org/deeplinks/2013/06/response-nsa-we-need-new-church-commission-and-we-need-it-now.

122   **After the Snowden leaks, I myself went:** *Terms and Conditions May Apply* (documentary), directed by Cullen Hoback (Los Angeles: Hyrax Films, 2013).

123   **In the study using the Stroop test:** Nemeth, Mosier, and Chiles, "When Convergent Thought Improves Performance."

123   **In a different but related study:** Randall S. Peterson and Charlan J. Nemeth, "Focus Versus Flexibility: Majority and Minority Influence Can Both Improve Performance," *Personality and Social Psychology Bulletin* 22, no. 1 (1996): 14–23.

125   **Their performance time was better than in any other condition:** Ibid.

127   **The study used an old method:** Nemeth and Kwan, "Originality of Word Associations."

129   **We were able to calculate the originality:** Leo Postman and Geoffrey Keppel, *Norms of Word Association* (New York: Academic Press, 1970).

130   **From the inception of brainstorming by Alex Osborn:** Alex F. Osborn, *Applied Imagination: Principles and Procedures of Creative Thinking* (New York: Scribner, 1958).

130   **People have argued over whether brainstorming:** Donald W. Taylor, Paul C. Berry, and Clifford H. Block, "Does Group Participation When Using Brainstorming Facilitate or Inhibit Creative Thinking?" *Administrative Science Quarterly* 6 (1958): 22–47. For thoughtful reviews and discussion, see Paul B. Paulus and Vincent R. Brown, "Enhancing Ideational Creativity in Groups: Lessons Learned from Research on Brainstorming," in *Group Creativity: Innovation Through Collaboration*, edited by Paul B. Paulus and Bernard A. Nijstad (New York: Oxford University

Press, 2003), 110–136; Scott G. Isaksen, "A Review of Brainstorming Research: Six Critical Issues for Inquiry," Monograph 303 (Buffalo, NY: Creative Problem Solving Group, Creative Research Unit, June 1998).

130   **We did this study the hard way:** Charlan J. Nemeth et al., "The Liberating Role of Conflict in Group Creativity: A Study in Two Countries," *European Journal of Social Psychology* 34, no. 4 (2004): 365–374.

132   **there is thoughtful research on the topic:** Vincent Brown and Paul B. Paulus, "A Simple Dynamic Model of Social Factors in Group Brainstorming," *Small Group Research* 27, no. 1 (1996): 91–114; Wolfgang Stroebe and Michael Diehl, "Why Groups Are Less Effective Than Their Members: On Productivity Losses in Idea-Generating Groups," *European Review of Social Psychology* 5, no. 1 (1994): 271–303.

132   **The popular press is now considering how criticism:** Rochelle Bailis, "Brainstorming Doesn't Work: Do This Instead," *Forbes*, October 8, 2014; Jonah Lehrer, "Groupthink: The Brainstorming Myth," *The New Yorker*, January 30, 2012.

CHAPTER 6: GROUP DECISIONS: OFTEN IN ERROR, NEVER IN DOUBT

139   **a way that "strains" for consensus:** Irving L. Janis, *Victims of Groupthink: A Psychological Study of Foreign Decisions and Fiascoes* (Boston: Houghton Mifflin, 1972).

139   **One of the best-known decision fiascoes:** "Bay of Pigs Invasion," *History*, www.history.com/topics/cold-war/bay-of-pigs-invasion (accessed December 23, 2016).

140   **"the mode of thinking . . . when concurrence-seeking":** Irving Janis, "Groupthink," *Psychology Today* (November 1971): 43.

140   **Janis popularized the term in his book:** Janis, *Victims of Groupthink.* The term "groupthink" originally is credited to William H. Whyte Jr., but it was popularized by Janis.

141   **In 1961, the decision was made:** "The Bay of Pigs Invasion Begins," *History*, www.history.com/this-day-in-history/the-bay-of-pigs-invasion-begins (accessed December 23, 2016).

141   **"immediately came under heavy fire":** John F. Kennedy Presi-

dential Library and Museum, "The Bay of Pigs," www.jfklibrary
.org/JFK/JFK-in-History/The-Bay-of-Pigs.aspx.

141 **In the aftermath, the US government was publicly embarrassed:** William M. LeoGrande, "Getting to Maybe: Next Steps
in Normalizing US-Cuba Relations," *World Politics Review*, August 11, 2015, www.worldpoliticsreview.com/articles/16434
/getting-to-maybe-next-steps-in-normalizing-u-s-cuba-relations.

142 **"How could I have been so stupid":** Robert Dallek, "Bay of Pigs:
Newly Revealed CIA Documents Expose Blunders," *Newsweek*,
August 14, 2011.

142 **subsequent research has shown inconsistent results:** Won-Woo
Park, "A Review of Research on Groupthink," *Journal of Behav-
ioral Decision Making* 3, no. 4 (1990): 229–245.

143 **"the women are strong":** Garrison Keillor, "National Geo-
graphic: In Search of Lake Wobegon," December 2000, www
.garrisonkeillor.com/national-geographic-in-search-of-lake
-wobegon/.

143 **the president and his advisers were so sure:** Peter Wyden, *Bay
of Pigs: The Untold Story* (New York: Simon & Schuster: 1979).

144 **"You may be right or you may be wrong":** Arthur M. Schlesinger
Jr., *A Thousand Days: John F. Kennedy in the White House* (Boston: Houghton Mifflin, 1965), 259.

144 **"I bitterly reproached myself":** Ibid., 250.

144 **"development of group norms that bolster":** Irving Janis,
"Groupthink" (early draft), https://department.monm.edu/cata
/McGaan/Classes/INTG415/Group-think.pdf.

144 **the research does seem to support the notion that a directed
leader:** Park, "A Review of Research on Groupthink."

145 **This was shown by norms that group members agree:** Janis,
"Groupthink" (early draft).

147 **Hundreds of studies have documented the fact:** David G. Myers and Helmut Lamm, "The Polarizing Effect of Group Discussion," *American Scientist* 63, no. 3 (1975): 297–303.

147 **this was found in studies on risk-taking:** James A. Stoner, "A
Comparison of Individual and Group Decision Involving Risk,"
unpublished master's thesis, Massachusetts Institute of Tech-
nology; Nathan Kogan and Michael A. Wallach, "Risk-taking as

a Function of the Situation, the Person, and the Group," in *New Directions in Psychology*, vol. 3, edited by T. M. Newcomb (New York: Holt, 1967).

148   **Either way, group discussion led them to become:** James A. F. Stoner, "Risky and Cautious Shifts in Group Decisions: The Influence of Widely Held Values," *Journal of Experimental Social Psychology* 4, no. 4 (1968): 442–459; Colin Fraser, Celia Gouge, and Michael Billig, "Risky Shifts, Cautious Shifts, and Group Polarization," *European Journal of Social Psychology* 1, no. 1 (1971): 7–30.

149   **a group might be only three people:** Fraser, Gouge, and Billig, "Risky Shifts, Cautious Shifts, and Group Polarization."

149   **studies conducted in France in the 1960s:** Serge Moscovici and Marisa Zavalloni, "The Group as a Polarizer of Attitudes," *Journal of Personality and Social Psychology* 12, no. 2 (1969): 125–135.

149   **Other studies corroborated this tendency:** David G. Myers and George D. Bishop, "Discussion Effects on Racial Attitudes," *Science* 169 (1970): 778–789; Helmut Lamm and David G. Myers, "Group-Induced Polarization of Attitudes and Behavior," in *Advances in Experimental Social Psychology*, edited by Leonard Berkowitz (San Diego, CA: Academic Press, 1978), 145–195.

150   **Citizens were encouraged to eat organ meats:** Cari Romm, "The World War II Campaign to Bring Organ Meats to the Dinner Table," *The Atlantic*, September 25, 2014.

150   **Compared to the lecture method:** Kurt Lewin, *Field Theory in Social Science: Selected Theoretical Papers* (New York: Harper & Row, 1951).

151   **Two prevailing theories have tried to explain:** Eugene Burnstein and Amiram Vinokur, "Persuasive Argumentation and Social Comparison as Determinants of Attitude Polarization," *Journal of Experimental Social Psychology* 13, no. 4 (1977): 315–332.

151   **The other theory is "social comparison" theory:** David G. Myers and Helmut Lamm, "The Group Polarization Phenomenon," *Psychological Bulletin* 83, no. 4 (1976): 602–627.

152   **The debates between the two theories:** Daniel J. Isenberg, "Group Polarization: A Critical Review and Meta-Analysis,"

Journal of Personality and Social Psychology 50, no. 6 (1986): 1141–1151.

152 **An early study by Garold Stasser and William Titus demonstrated:** Garold Stasser and William Titus, "Pooling of Unshared Information in Group Decision Making: Biased Information Sampling During Discussion," *Journal of Personality and Social Psychology* 48, no. 6 (1985): 1467–1478.

154 **There might be several reasons for why the group members:** Garold Stasser and Zachary Birchmeier, "Group Creativity and Collective Choice," in *Group Creativity: Innovation Through Collaboration,* edited by Paul B. Paulus and Bernard A. Nijstad (Oxford: Oxford University Press, 2003), 85–109.

154 **One study showed this proportion to be as strong:** Garold Stasser, Laurie A. Taylor, and Coleen Hanna, "Information Sampling in Structured and Unstructured Discussions of Three- and Six-Person Groups," *Journal of Personality and Social Psychology* 57, no. 1 (1989): 67–78.

154 **This same pattern has been found in a study:** James R. Larson, Caryn Christensen, Ann S. Abbott, and Timothy M. Franz, "Diagnosing Groups: Charting the Flow of Information in Medical Decision-Making Teams," *Journal of Personality and Social Psychology* 71, no. 2 (1996): 315–330.

155 **Subsequent research shows that unique information:** Gwen M. Wittenbaum and Ernest S. Park, "The Collective Preference for Shared Information," *Current Directions in Psychological Science* 10, no. 2 (2001): 70–73.

155 **This diagnosis led to a very different decision:** Thank you, Jesse Dohemann.

156 **Schlesinger did not share his unique information:** Schlesinger, *A Thousand Days.*

157 **A meta-analysis of sixty-five studies:** Li Lu, Y. Connie Yuan, and Poppy Lauretta McLeod, "Twenty-Five Years of Hidden Profiles in Group Decision Making: A Meta-Analysis," *Personality and Social Psychology Review* 16, no. 1 (2012): 54–75.

158 **They had a chance to use what they learned:** US Department of State, Office of the Historian, "The Cuban Missile Crisis,

October 1962," October 31, 2013, https://history.state.gov
/milestones/1961–1968/cuban-missile-crisis.

159   **someone suggested an alternative to invasion:** Morton T. Hansen, "How John F. Kennedy Changed Decision Making for Us
All," *Harvard Business Review,* November 22, 2013, https://hbr
.org/2013/11/how-john-f-kennedy-changed-decision-making.

159   **Other changes in the decision-making process reportedly:** Ibid.

159   **Martin Hansen, writing in the *Harvard Business Review:*** Ibid.

160   **"relax the forces pulling on the ends of the rope":** US Department of State, Office of the Historian, "The Cuban Missile Crisis."

161   **"combination of toughness and restraint":** Schlesinger, *A Thousand Days,* 841.

161   **corporate cultures can aid good decision-making:** Charlan
Nemeth, "Managing Innovation: When Less Is More," *California
Management Review* 40 (1997): 59–74.

CHAPTER 7: BETTER DECISIONS: DISSENT, DIVERSITY, AND DEVIL'S ADVOCATES

164   **"evaluate risks and benefits with equal vigor":** *Harvard Business
Review,* Daniel Kahneman, and Ram Charan, *HBR's 10 Must
Reads on Making Smart Decisions* (Boston: Harvard Business
School Publishing, 2013), jacket cover.

165   **In 1995, the trial of the century was held:** Greg Braxton, "'O. J.:
Trial of the Century' Revisits Murder Case as It Unfolded," *Los
Angeles Times,* June 12, 2014.

165   **Racial tensions ran high throughout the trial:** David Margolick,
"Victims Put Up Long Fight, a Witness for Simpson Says," *New
York Times,* August 11, 1995.

166   **On October 3, 1995, after nine months of testimony:** Jim Hill,
"Emotions High over Simpson Verdict," *CNN,* October 8, 1995,
www.cnn.com/US/OJ/daily/9510/10–08/.

166   **He moved to Florida where, by law:** B. Drummond Ayres
Jr., "Jury Decides Simpson Must Pay $25 Million in Punitive
Award," *New York Times,* February 11, 1997.

166   **The two cases differed in a number of respects:** "How O. J.
Simpson's Criminal, Civil Trials Differed," *Seattle Times,* February 5, 1997.

167 **for what researchers call in-group favoritism:** Jacob M. Rabbie and Murray Horwitz, "Arousal of Ingroup-Outgroup Bias by a Chance Win or Loss," *Journal of Personality and Social Psychology* 13, no. 3 (1969): 269–277; Henri Tajfel, "Social Psychology of Intergroup Relations," *Annual Review of Psychology* 33, no. 1 (1982): 1–39.

167 **when people were brought into a laboratory:** Henri Tajfel, "Experiment in Intergroup Discrimination," *Scientific American* 223, no. 5 (1970): 96–102.

168 **The city of Miami still remembers the 1980 case:** Wilson Sayre, "Smoldering Liberty City: Remembering the McDuffie Riots," *WLRN*, May 17, 2015, http://wlrn.org/post/smoldering -liberty-city-remembering-mcduffie-riots.

168 **"As many as a dozen officers beat him":** David Smiley, "McDuffie Riots: Revisiting, Retelling Story—35 Years Later," *Miami Herald*, May 16, 2015.

168 **By some accounts, the ensuing three days:** "McDuffie Riots: Eerie Scene from Miami Race Riot of 1980," *Huffington Post*, May 29, 2013, www.huffingtonpost.com/2013/05/29/mcduffie -riots-miami_n_3353719.html.

169 **There were not only protests but rioting:** Larry Buchanan et al., "Q&A: What Happened in Ferguson?" *New York Times*, August 10, 2015.

169 **"lacks prosecutive merit and should be closed":** US Department of Justice, *Department of Justice Report Regarding the Criminal Investigation into the Shooting Death of Michael Brown by Ferguson, Missouri Police Officer Darren Wilson*, March 4, 2015, 86, www.justice.gov/sites/default/files/opa/press-releases /attachments/2015/03/04/doj_report_on_shooting_of_michael _brown_1.pdf.

171 **the research shows mixed results:** Susan E. Jackson, Karen E. May, and Kristina Whitney, "Understanding the Dynamics of Diversity in Decision-Making Teams," in *Team Effectiveness and Decision Making in Organizations*, edited by Richard A. Guzzo, Eduardo Salas, and Associates (San Francisco: Jossey-Bass, 1995); Katherine Y. Williams and Charles A. O'Reilly, "Demography and Diversity in Organizations: A Review of 40 Years

of Research," *Research in Organizational Behavior* 20 (1998): 77–140.

171 **Studies show that diversity of demographics:** Williams and O'Reilly, "Demography and Diversity in Organizations."

171 **Since there is repeated evidence that similarity:** Miller McPherson, Lynn Smith-Lovin, and James M. Cook, "Birds of a Feather: Homophily in Social Networks," *Annual Review of Sociology* 27 (2001): 415–444.

171 **the numerous studies and even meta-analyses of the research:** Clint A. Bowers, James A. Pharmer, and Eduardo Salas, "When Member Homogeneity Is Needed in Work Teams: A Meta-Analysis," *Small Group Research* 31, no. 3 (2000): 305–327; Susan E. Jackson, Joan F. Brett, Valerie I. Sessa, Dawn M. Cooper, Johan A. Julin, and Karl Peyronnin, "Some Differences Make a Difference: Individual Dissimilarity and Group Heterogeneity as Correlates of Recruitment, Promotions, and Turnover," *Journal of Applied Psychology* 76, no. 5 (1991): 675.

171 **"neither diversity on readily observable attributes":** Daan van Knippenberg, Carsten K. W. De Dreu, and Astrid C. Homan, "Work Group Diversity and Group Performance: An Integrative Model and Research Agenda," *Journal of Applied Psychology* 89, no. 6 (2004): 1009.

172 **"whether increased diversity actually adds":** Williams and O'Reilly, "Demography and Diversity in Organizations."

172 **"team of rivals":** Doris Kearns Goodwin, *Team of Rivals: The Political Genius of Abraham Lincoln* (New York: Simon & Schuster, 2005).

173 **"You're not looking for people who are just like you":** Carrie Schwab-Pomerantz, interview with the author, June 2015.

173 **one of her favorite books is *Team of Rivals*:** Carrie Schwab-Pomerantz, "Being a Leader Isn't About You—It's About Them," *LinkedIn*, July 6, 2015, www.linkedin.com/pulse/how-i-lead-being-leader-isnt-you-its-them-carrie-schwab-pomerantz.

173 **Whitney Mortimer, partner and chief marketing officer:** "Program for International Women's Forum Northern California," IDEO offices, San Francisco August 3, 2015.

174   **So has his senior vice president of marketing:** Nora Denzel, interview with the author, February 10, 2014.

174   **Catherine Lelong, who worked at Wolff Olins:** Catherine LeLong, interview with the author, August 11, 2014.

175   **She may be one of the most open people:** Jenny Johnson, interviews with the author, May 16, 2014, and June 15, 2014.

178   **a field study in which groups of four or five:** Linn Van Dyne and Richard Saavedra, "A Naturalistic Minority Influence Experiment: Effects on Divergent Thinking, Conflict, and Originality in Work-Groups," *British Journal of Social Psychology* 35, no. 1 (1996): 151–167.

178   **"identified a large number of alternatives":** Ibid., 158.

178   **One of the most ambitious naturalistic studies:** Robert S. Dooley and Gerald E. Fryxell, "Attaining Decision Quality and Commitment from Dissent: The Moderating Effects of Loyalty and Competence in Strategic Decision-Making Teams," *Academy of Management Journal* 42, no. 4 (1999): 389–402.

178   **"they work with more, rather than less":** Kathleen M. Eisenhardt, Jean L. Kahwajy, and L. J. Bourgeois III, "How Management Teams Can Have a Good Fight," *Harvard Business Review* (July-August 1997).

179   **Dissent has been found to increase:** Deborah H. Gruenfeld, "Status, Ideology, and Integrative Complexity on the US Supreme Court: Rethinking the Politics of Political Decision Making," *Journal of Personality and Social Psychology* 68, no. 1 (1995): 5–20.

179   **This concept is akin to divergent thinking:** Peter Suedfeld, Philip E. Tetlock, and Siegfried Streufert, "Conceptual/Integrative Complexity," in *Motivation and Personality: Handbook of Thematic Content Analysis,* edited by Charles P. Smith et al. (New York: Cambridge University Press, 1992), 393–400.

179   **One study of Supreme Court decisions:** Gruenfeld, "Status, Ideology, and Integrative Complexity."

179   **"to go along and to get along":** Dale Carnegie, *How to Win Friends and Influence People* (New York: Simon & Schuster, 1936).

180   **"not get out of the angioplasty business":** Jeffrey A. Sonnenfeld, "What Makes Great Boards Great," *Harvard Business Review* 80, no. 9 (2002): 106–113.

181   **Recent books like Tom Kelley's *The Ten Faces of Innovation*:** Tom Kelley, with Jonathan Littman, *The Ten Faces of Innovation: IDEO's Strategies for Beating the Devil's Advocate and Driving Creativity Throughout Your Organization* (Garden City, NY: Doubleday, 2005).

181   **Thus, in 1587, they instituted a practice:** Ricard Burtsell, "Advocatus Diaboli," in *The Catholic Encyclopedia*, vol. 1 (New York: Robert Appleton Co., 1907), available at *New Advent*, www.newadvent.org/cathen/01168b.htm.

182   **the devil's advocate is but one mechanism:** Rebecca Leung, "The Debate over Sainthood," *CBS News*, October 19, 2003, www.cbsnews.com/news/the-debate-over-sainthood/.

182   **Devil's advocate was the antidote favored by Irving Janis:** Janis and Mann, *Decision Making*.

182   **"evaluate risks and benefits with equal vigor":** *Harvard Business Review* et al., *HBR's 10 Must Reads on Making Smart Decisions*, jacket cover.

182   **Available research on the devil's advocate technique:** Richard A. Cosier, "The Effects of Three Potential Aids for Making Strategic Decisions on Prediction Accuracy," *Organizational Behavior and Human Performance* 22, no. 2 (1978): 295–306; Ian I. Mitroff and Richard O. Mason, "The Metaphysics of Policy and Planning: A Reply to Cosier," *Academy of Management Review* 6, no. 4 (1981): 649–651.

183   **So, too, can its sister technique, dialectical inquiry:** Gary Katzenstein, "The Debate on Structured Debate: Toward a Unified Theory," *Organizational Behavior and Human Decision Processes* 66, no. 3 (1996): 316–332.

183   **which has shown some promise in lowering bias:** Charles G. Lord, Mark R. Lepper, and Elizabeth Preston, "Considering the Opposite: A Corrective Strategy for Social Judgment," *Journal of Personality and Social Psychology* 47, no. 6 (1984): 1231–1243; Edward R. Hirt, Frank R. Kardes, and Keith D. Markman, "Activating a Mental Simulation Mind-set Through Generation

of Alternatives: Implications for Debiasing in Related and Un-related Domains," *Journal of Experimental Social Psychology* 40, no. 3 (2004): 374–383.

184 **It no longer featured the robust conflict:** Charlan Nemeth, "Interactions Between Jurors as a Function of Majority vs. Unanimity Decision Rules," *Journal of Applied Social Psychology* 7 (1977): 38–56.

185 **I undertook the first study when three graduate students:** Charlan Jeanne Nemeth et al., "Improving Decision Making by Means of Dissent," *Journal of Applied Social Psychology* 31, no. 1 (2001): 48–58.

186 **This technique has been found to be very useful in tracking:** John T. Cacioppo and Richard E. Petty, "Social Psychological Procedures for Cognitive Response Assessment: The Thought-Listing Technique," *Cognitive Assessment* (1981): 309–342.

187 **Our findings had shown that there is a reason to be cautious:** Dorothy Leonard and Walter Swap, *When Sparks Fly: Igniting Creativity in Groups* (Boston: Harvard Business School Press, 1999).

187 **A second study took this a step further:** Charlan Nemeth, Keith Brown, and John Rogers, "Devil's Advocate Versus Authentic Dissent: Stimulating Quantity and Quality," *European Journal of Social Psychology* 31 (2001): 707–720.

190 **a pumped-up version of devil's advocate:** Cass R. Sunstein and Reid Hastie, "How to Defeat Groupthink: Five Solutions," *Fortune*, January 13, 2015.

192 **I had the occasion to interview its founder:** Ankur Luthra and Brendan Nemeth, interview with the author, October 17, 2016.

193 **if Finchwood wants to buy stock XYZ:** "Short selling is the sale of a security that is not owned by the seller, or that the seller has borrowed. Short selling is motivated by the belief that a security's price will decline, enabling it to be bought back at a lower price to make a profit." "Short Selling," *Investopedia*, www.investopedia.com/terms/s/shortselling.asp (accessed December 23, 2016).

195   **An international icon, she had been widely applauded:** "Mother
      Teresa," *Wikipedia,* https://en.wikipedia.org/wiki/Mother_Teresa
      (accessed December 23, 2016).

195   **That fierce critic was none other than Christopher Hitchens:**
      "Christopher Hitchens," *Wikipedia,* https://en.wikipedia.org
      /wiki/Christopher_Hitchens (accessed December 23, 2016).

195   **Hitchens had criticized Mother Teresa:** Christopher Hitchens,
      "Mommie Dearest," *Slate,* October 20, 2003, www.slate.com
      /articles/news_and_politics/fighting_words/2003/10/mommie
      _dearest.html.

195   **"his argument was irrelevant":** Leung, "The Debate over
      Sainthood."

CHAPTER 8: CONCLUSIONS

199   **For example, one shows a boss:** "Dissent Cartoons and Com-
      ics," *CartoonStock,* www.cartoonstock.com/directory/d/dissent
      .asp (accessed December 23, 2016).

199   **"I encourage dissent":** Harry Hongda Wu and George
      Vecsey, *Troublemaker: One Man's Crusade Against China's Cru-
      elty* (West Palm Beach, FL: NewsMax Media, 2002), 49–55.

200   **"A lone dissenter risks his life":** "15 Rare Historical Photos
      You've Never Seen Before!" *BoredomBash,* December 5, 2014,
      http://boredombash.com/15-rare-historical-photos/.

203   **"The only way I can get you to do anything":** Carnegie, *How to
      Win Friends and Influence People,* 19.

203   **Most, but not all, of the research shows some value:** Cosier,
      "The Effects of Three Potential Aids."

204   **the devil's advocate does not have the vigor:** Nemeth et al.,
      "Devil's Advocate Versus Authentic Dissent."

204   **these techniques may have unintended negative consequences:**
      Nemeth et al., "Improving Decision Making by Means of Dissent."

205   **whose mission is to advance health, education, and equity:** De-
      nise Dunning, interview with the author, December 2016.

205   **She doesn't pursue these goals by building schools:** Denise
      Dunning, interview with the author, March 26, 2015.

206   **a young woman from Malawi:** Reception for Let Girls Lead,
      March 18, 2015, San Francisco.

207 **Memory had started on her journey:** Joyce Hackel, "Memory Banda Escaped Child Marriage in Malawi, but Her 11-Year-Old Sister Wasn't So Lucky," *PRI*, March 12, 2015, www.pri.org /stories/2015-03-12/memory-banda-escaped-child-marriage -malawi-her-11-year-old-sister-wasnt-so-lucky.

207 **Malawi raised the legal age of marriage:** Denise Dunning and Joyce Mkandawire, "How Girl Activists Helped to Ban Child Marriage in Malawi," *The Guardian*, February 26, 2015.

209 **people need to feel safe in expressing dissent:** Nemeth, "Managing Innovation."

209 **Such a group has a chance to become a "hot group":** Harold J. Leavitt and Jean Lipmen-Blumen, "Hot Groups," *Harvard Business Review* (July/August 1995), https://hbr.org/1995/07 /hot-groups.

209 **Jane Wales, CEO of the World Affairs Council:** Jane Wales, interview with the author, March 2014.

211 **Dale Carnegie advised that we be nice:** Carnegie, *How to Win Friends and Influence People.*

211 **Osborn, who gave us the four brainstorming rules:** Osborn, *Applied Imagination.*

211 **as studies in the United States and France have confirmed:** Nemeth et al., "The Liberating Role of Conflict in Group Creativity."

212 **If the dissent is correct:** This is essentially a paraphrase from John Stuart Mill's book *On Liberty:* "If the opinion is right, they are deprived of the opportunity of exchanging error for truth: if wrong, they lose, what is almost as great a benefit, the clearer perception and livelier impression of truth, produced by its collision with error." Mill, *On Liberty* (New York: Simon & Brown, 2012), 17–18.

212 **scandals such as the rogue trader known as "the London Whale":** Patricia Hurtado, "The London Whale," *Bloomberg*, April 23, 2015, www.bloombergview.com/quicktake/the-london-whale.

213 **risk limits were breached more than three hundred times:** Ibid.

214 **"The beginning of thought is in disagreement":** Eric Hoffer, *The Passionate State of Mind: And Other Aphorisms* (Perennial Library, 1955).

INDEX

CHARLAN NEMETH is a professor in the Department of Psychology at the University of California, Berkeley. She lives in San Francisco.